The ABCs of
Boat Camping

Gordon Groene & Janet Groene

By the same authors

Cooking on the Go
Living Aboard Your RV
Cooking Aboard Your RV
Country Roads of Ohio
Natural Wonders of Ohio
Florida Under Sail
Fifty-two Florida Weekends
Natural Wonders of Georgia

The ABCs of Boat Camping

Gordon Groene & Janet Groene

S

Sheridan House

First published 1994
by Sheridan House Inc.
145 Palisade Street
Dobbs Ferry, NY   10522

Library of Congress Cataloging-in-Publication Data

Groene, Janet.
    The ABCs of boat camping / Janet Groene and Gordon Groene.
        p. cm.
    Includes bibliographical references (p.) and index.
    ISBN 0-924486-59-7 : $16.50
    1. Boats and boating. 2. Camping. I. Groene, Gordon.
    II. Title.
    GV775.G76 1994
    797.1--dc20   94-8567
                                                      CIP

ISBN 0-924486-59-7

Printed in the United States of America

Design by Sarah K. Myers

Table of Contents

Introduction

So your boat isn't a yacht complete with galley, head, hanging lockers, and bunks? We don't see this as a minus. We see it as a magic carpet that is small enough and light enough to take you into the most secret, shallow coves.

Your boat can carry you up creeks that shrink to mere slivers, can send you streaking down raging rivers. Small sail- or paddle-powered craft take you through sweet, dark waters where outboards are not permitted. Robust little powerboats whisk you across the Gulf Stream to have lunch at Bimini and a night under the stars at Honeymoon Harbor beach.

Best of all, this little boat is affordable enough to take you right now on the most exciting overnight adventures. You may camp on your own private sandspit or sandy beach. Or you ride at anchor, far from land's heat and bugs, while gentle waves rock you to sleep.

There is nothing quite like morning mist on the water. You're the first angler on the scene because you slept there all night. It's chilly and utterly soundless, perhaps a bit too cold and damp when you first shrug off the sleeping bag. Then the sun rises out of a wet horizon and glows warmer as you brew a cup of coffee. You realize how rich your life can be with a small craft and a few scraps of canvas.

This book is for rag sailors and stinkpotters, paddlers and rowers, scullers and floaters. It is for those who love the silent sports and for those whose shrieking airboats could wake the dead. It is for river runners, swamp rats, old salts, and lake lappers.

It is for everyone who wants to stay out all night, all week, all season, in a boat that in itself is not quite enough to provide the comforts of home. It is about boat camping.

Even some of the smallest runabouts can sleep two aboard, either in a V-berth forward in a cuddy cabin or on the two bunks that are formed when four fore-and-aft seats are folded down.

We assume that some of you will sleep aboard and some ashore. Most boat campers use some sort of canvas tent or enclosure on or near the boat, though sometimes we utilize shoreside campground shelters such as KOA Kamping Kabins.

The galley we envision must be portable, to be set up on deck, in the cockpit, on the dock, or at a shoreside campsite. Any bathing will be done in the water, in campground or marina showers, or with portable facilities. Some of you will have portable toilets to be used on board or on land.

Boat camping is camping without wheels and boating to the live-aboard max. It takes many forms, but all of them have hows, dos, and don'ts in common. Come and learn about it all. Come and celebrate this unique sport with us.

I
The Dream

1

Whale-Sized Adventures, Minnow-Sized Boats

Few of us will experience daring boat-camping heroics, but reading about them is entertaining and inspiring. Stories like these show what can be done with a small boat, a few scraps of canvas, and a yen for adventure.

One of our favorite books, *Tinkerbelle* (Harper and Row), tells of Robert Manry's record-setting trans-Atlantic voyage in what was, at the time, the smallest sailboat to have crossed that ocean. Most people remember the story of Manry's lone ocean crossing. We were more beguiled by other portions of the book, which describe how the Manry family used the boat as a camper on the Great Lakes. The Manrys simply drove their tow car, with the sailboat on its trailer, into a campground and used the boat as their motor home. They sailed by day, retrieved the boat at night, and went back to their RV campsite.

We pass along the Manry story and the others that follow in hopes that you'll find more and better ways to boat camp near home and in all the world's lakes and streams.

Old Favorites

Theodore Roosevelt and his 16 paddlers boat camped for 42 nights as they followed the River of Doubt from its source to where it joins the Amazon River in Brazil. His report is available in the National Geographic Society archives.

• Enid Wolf wrote a cruising manual for women in the 1950s, *A Boating We Will Go* (McGraw-Hill). It tells how a family of two adults and four children cruised in a 22-foot power boat. If Wolf could do it with the primitive gear of the '50s, boat camping in a tiny boat with four kids should be a snap today!

• Another old book, *Survival of the Bark Canoe*, by John McPhee (Farrar, Straus and Giroux), is a loving tribute to canoes that were used by native Americans. The author traveled with canoe builder Henri Vaillancourt, who used only authentic native materials to create bark canoes. The two men canoe camped for 150 miles through the Maine woods.

• In *The Search for the Pink-Headed Duck* (Houghton Mifflin) Rory Nugent tells of his search for a duck that was thought to be extinct. Boat camping in a 13-foot skiff, he was the first person to paddle the Brahmaputra River from Burma to Bangladesh. His tent was a plastic rectangle stretched over split bamboo, which left eight inches of his feet exposed to the elements. His stove was an old oilcan he had crimped and bent to hold a cooking pot.

• Jeff MacInnis set out from Inuvik in Canada's Northwest Territories in July 1986 to sail the Northwest Passage in a Hobie Cat in what must have been one of the most challenging, exhilarating, and *cold* boat-camping expeditions of our century. On most nights he made camp; occasionally he took shelter in remote DEW Line stations. The trip took two seasons, but he reached his goal—one that to this day eludes many powerful expeditions equipped with icebreaker hulls, sophisticated electronics, and other luxuries.

MacInnis, with his photographer Mike Beedell, towed the 700-pound Hobie-18 4,000 miles north from Toronto and simply launched the boat at the end of the road, the way most other boat campers do. The team carried 1½ pounds of food per person per day, plus a tent and mummy sleeping bags. They wore one-piece Gore-Tex DUI (Diving Unlimited International) diving dry suits with neck and wrist seals, and they sailed with emergency locator beacons strapped to their bodies and inflatable one-man survival seats (a sort of mini liferaft) strapped to their backs.

• Canoe campers may want to seek out another old book, *Down the Wild River North* (Little, Brown and Company). The author and her two daughters, aged 12 and 14, spent two summers taking a 20-foot freight canoe down the Peace and Mackenzie rivers in the Arctic.

With a very small boat and budget, you can probe some of the world's best boating waters. *Coleman*

Marathons and More

Here are some other firsthand reports you might ponder when you're thinking about boat camping in ordinary or extraordinary ways.

• Rowing across the Atlantic Ocean may not qualify as boat camping because the two rowers, Chay Blyth and John Ridgway, "camped" entirely on board for the two months it took them to row from Cape Cod to Ireland, but the trip was remarkable nonetheless. Seventy years earlier, in 1896, Frank Samuelson and George Harbo had accomplished the same incredible feat.

• Joe Skorupa, boating and outdoors editor of *Popular Mechanics*, took a 20-foot bass boat from New Orleans to St. Paul, Minnesota, an adventure that was reported in the December 1992 issue of the magazine. We received a reprint of the write-up from Bayliner, makers of the Astro DCX boat that was home for a week to Skorupa and his copilot, Jim Youngs. Skorupa and Youngs covered 1,734 miles at speeds up to 60 mph, went through 25 locks, used 594.4 gallons of gas and 13 gallons of oil in their Mariner V-6 200 EFI, and had the time of their lives.

By car the 6½-day trip would have taken 24 hours; by air the 1,250 miles would have been covered between breakfast and lunch. "Given the chance to do it all over again," Skorupa wrote, "we'd pick the river route every time. Even in a bass boat."

• Canoeing on the Mississippi and Missouri rivers is described by Nicholas Francis and William Butcher in their book, *Mississippi Madness* (Sheridan House).

• Would boat camping be simpler if you could hack out enough chunks of snow each night to make a snug igloo? John Bockstoce, historian and archeologist, wrote *Arctic Passages* (William Morrow) about his extraordinary 3,500-mile journey through the Northwest Passage. Much of the trip was made in an umiak that Bockstoce turned over on shore each night to provide shelter. On another leg Bockstoce used a 20-foot flat-stern canoe, which he trailered to the Tanana River, outside Fairbanks, and took down the Yukon River to the Bering Sea. His cargo was:

> "Lumber [for rebuilding the umiak he would use later], our grub box, a Coleman campstove, the outboard [motors] as well as spare parts and propellers, a tent and sleeping bags, a couple of reindeer skins for mattresses, ten five-gallon gasoline jugs and three fuel tanks, a shovel, an ax, and a handful of tools...."

The book is a must read for armchair sailors and for anyone who wants to boat camp the high Arctic.

• In 1993 Steve Wainwright, a writer for the *Seattle Times*, reported on a 12-day, 100-mile canoe trip that he, four other adults, and three children, aged 2, 4, and 14, took in the Everglades. Unlike some other stories of great expeditions, this was tame and family-oriented fare that any of us could identify with. That's what makes it so appealing. The three-canoe flotilla was the project of Earth Knack, a Boulder-based company that dreams up adventure trips in the world's great wildernesses.

To find outfitters, guides, and instructors who can take you on your first canoe, kayak, or other boat-camping adventure, read *Eco-Vacations* by Evelyn Kaye. It's published by Blue Penguin Publications (800–800–8147 or 201–461–6918).

• In the 1980s William Sanders of Little Rock, Arkansas, boat camped the 67-mile Big Piney Creek in the Ozarks in a 9-foot inflatable Sea Eagle canoe that weighed only 18 pounds. He carried it and all his other gear in a backpack, riding buses and hitchhiking to get from home to the river.

• Michael and Ida Little canoe camped the Caribbean island of Martinique in the late 1980s in a 17-foot Old Town canoe with sail rig and a snap-on cover. Their cruise began aboard Holland America's luxurious *Rotterdam*, which carried them in swank, air-conditioned comfort to the steam heat of Martinique. It took a bit of adjusting to get over the culture shock, but the Littles were soon off on a fabulous adventure.

Their supplies included sleeping pads, an Optimus kerosene stove, a kerosene lantern, a five-gallon water jug, 10 pounds of fruitcake, and a guitar. Their gear—including cameras, bedding, and papers—was safely packed in waterproof canoe bags. Their fresh foods came from native markets along the way.

The Littles found canoe camping in the Caribbean markedly different from their earlier cruise of the area in a 40-foot yacht. Canoe cruising allowed them to "surrender" themselves to Caribbean peoples and cultures without having to worry about the big investment that the 40-footer represented.

• Cruising 900 miles of the icy Labrador coast in an 18-foot skiff in the summer of 1980, Dave Getchell and Geoff Heath chose simple camping gear: a two-person tent, a gasoline stove, two pots plus a frying pan, and two sleeping bags each. Their engine was a Mariner 25, and they carried a 5-HP Suzuki as a spare. Their emergency supplies included an Emergency Position Indicating Radio Beacon (EPIRB), flares, and an international orange flag. They also added a rope ladder because they knew that, in these cold waters, hypothermia would quickly set in and make it impossible for them to climb back aboard without help. They rigged the ladder so that one end could be thrown over the side in an emergency.

They added a short, cold-molded wood deck to the bow of the 18-foot aluminum Lund skiff and extended that with a nylon canopy. The resulting area was large enough to provide shelter for the man who was off watch. On nights when there was no time, energy, or a space to put up their tent, it provided a snug sleeping area.

• Bonnie Hepburn found the Hobie Cat Sport Cruiser the ideal boat-camping rig for Baja California while she was testing the boat for *Hobie Hotline* magazine in 1992. Designed for cruising, this Hobie has lots of stowage space in the hulls and in the cabin, plus an optional tramp tent that Bonnie reported was about as big as a king-sized bed.

The team was equipped for shameless luxury: beach chairs, motor bracket and motor, fishing gear, wet suits, and even a sailboard. The Cat Cooler was crammed with 68 quarts of provisions, and Hepburn discovered that it also served as a perfect worktable on the beach. The team carried a folding shovel, which came in handy for digging clams and creating latrines, and they blessed the folding beach dolly that made it possible for them to drag the 21-foot boat well inland each night.

• Steve Gropp and Mary Pederson of Orcas Island, Washington, rowed a 16-foot open dory all the way around 250-mile-long Vancouver Island, British Columbia, in the summer of 1980. The boat, which had a small sail to take advantage of any following winds, also carried 800 feet of line, two anchors, and camping gear including a tent and sleeping bags. The boat-camping adventure of a lifetime took exactly 80 days, some of them spent rowing almost 30 miles and others spent holed up in their tent waiting for wet, violent weather to pass.

Is *your* story one we'll be reading next in a book or in one of the outdoor adventure magazines? We hope so!

2
Where to Go Boat Camping

Where should you boat camp? Where should you *not* go ashore and make camp?

At one extreme, we'd like to say that it's easier to apologize than to ask permission. However, to be on the safe side, we advise you to boat camp only in areas where it is expressly permitted. Somewhere between these two extremes lies a middle ground—pardon the pun—where you can find the most memorable boat camping in the world without spending a fortune or running afoul of the law.

To pitch a tent on Palm Beach just seaside of a multimillion-dollar mansion or on a patrolled beach at Daytona or Fort Lauderdale is to ask for trouble. To build a roaring driftwood fire anywhere is to call attention to yourself, even in places where camping is allowed, and perhaps to bring the law down on you for creating a fire hazard or a general nuisance.

Start out with a good attitude, a low profile, and a profound respect for the laws of man and nature. If you start a brushfire or disturb tender growth or turtle nests or fragile dunes, you are in violation of immutable natural laws.

Theoretically, most beaches and banks cannot be privately owned (although an angry landowner may well greet you with a shotgun if you set a toe over the high-water mark). Still, with prudence and planning, plus a little cunning and a touch of chutzpah, you can find a world of free, picture-pretty, waterfront campsites out there waiting for you.

Here's a sampling of some of the best boat-camping areas in North America. We caution you that the sources we list are only a first step in finding out about boat camping. You'll need to do a great deal of spadework on your own, because tourist-promotion agencies are trying to sell fishing charters, dude ranches, and hotel rooms. Rarely will they send you a brochure that tells you exactly how and where to pull your boat up onto the beach and stay rent free.

Brochures that cover boating or camping are available if you're persistent. However, slick brochures that tell you where you can boat camp in an unpeopled wilderness are almost impossible to come by.

Gather up all the information possible on boating and on camping, then put two and two together. As you assemble lists of boat-camping paradises, keep them as your own secret. Ours include a farmer's field along a wide place in a clear stream in downstate Illinois near the Indiana border, uninhabited cays in the Bahamas and Florida Keys, hundreds of gunkholes along the TVA lakes, and many more. Our list is still growing. Start yours today.

The Bahamas

A nation of 700 islands in a clear sea the color of Windex, the Bahamas is the finest cruising ground in the world. If you're looking for an exotic, foreign flavor within hours of U.S. shores, a climate that is mild all year long, a variety of protected or ocean sailing spots, and uncounted miles of deserted beaches, you'll find them all here. If you've only seen Nassau and Freeport, you haven't a clue as to what can be found in the islands.

Boat camping in the Bahamas won't be for everyone. You need a boat that is robust enough to take on the Gulf Stream (which can contain some of the roughest waters in the world) and other ocean passages within the Bahamas. You'll also need plenty of advance planning, so you'll have enough fuel and provisions, and an idea of what places on what islands are open to boat camping. The surest bets are islands that are completely uninhabited, although many inhabited islands have long stretches of unpeopled shores.

Absolutely indispensable is the *Yachtsman's Guide to the Bahamas,* a new edition of which is published each year by Tropic Isle Publishers, Inc., Box 610938, North Miami, Florida 33261–0938.

Everglades National Park, Florida

Silent, flat, and filled with seas of saw grass and sedges broken only by featureless forests, the Everglades keeps its mystique hidden from hurried travelers. It does, however, reveal its magic to boat campers who are willing to take the time and toil to probe its secret streams.

In other national parks, with their spectacular mountains and forests, the beauty leaps out and grabs you. In the Everglades, by contrast, the drama takes time to emerge from what at first appears to be miles of nothing but flat water and scrub growth. As it does, wonder turns to awe. Because much of the wildlife is most active at twilight and dawn, boat campers see the best of it, before day-trippers arrive and after they leave for their air-conditioned condos.

Pelicans dive-bomb boats out of nowhere, disappear into the dark water, and come up with a bill full of fish. At night nesting egrets turn whole islands white. Once, sitting at anchor in the early-morning calm, we watched as an osprey flapped overhead with an enormous snake in its mouth.

Alligators slither up to the boat, hoping for handouts. Turtles bask in the sun. Raccoons and deer steal to the water's edge for an early-morning drink. If you're lucky you may see rare species: Florida panthers, bald eagles, wood storks, manatees.

The largest subtropical wilderness in North America, the Everglades sprawl wetly over 2,200 square miles. You shouldn't go boat camping in the area without thorough planning and preparation. You need good charts, local advice from park rangers, and a tankerload of bug spray.

Major waterways are marked, but side channels wind on forever. It's an endless maze where the unwary can wind up aground in a dead end. The size of the Everglades alone is stunning. So is the variety of boating, which ranges from blackwater channels through forests of hardwood or mangrove, to white-sugar sand beaches better than any on the Riviera.

Camping is permitted on three islands in Florida Bay. Two of the islands have small docks and primitive toilets. The third, Carl Ross Key, has no facilities and is difficult to get to during low water, so it's a very private hideaway that is ideal for canoe or catamaran camping. Also available are "chickee," or palmetto-frond-hut, camping platforms with docks along Whitewater Bay and the Wilderness Waterway.

Charles Waterman, dean of outdoor writers and the author of numerous books on fishing and shooting, camped many miles in the Everglades with his wife, Debbie. Their equipment included a 16-foot aluminum boat with a plywood platform in the bow. By day it served as a fishing platform. At night the Watermans hung their gear in mangrove trees and set up a framed tent and sleeping bags on the platform. *Charles F. Waterman*

Fire is a special danger to the Everglades: one brushfire can destroy thousands of acres of this extremely fragile environment. Scrupulously observe whatever fire code is in effect during your visit.

The Everglades are best from October through April. In summer they're insufferably hot and buggy, although the wildlife show is different and often better. Crowds, rarely a problem in the remote areas favored by boat campers, are even less of a problem in summer. Not all facilities will be open, however.

For information about the Everglades' many boat-access sites on canals and levees throughout the southern part of the state, write to the South Florida Water Management District, P. O. Box V, West Palm Beach, Florida 33402.

For information about boating and camping in the national-park portion of the Everglades, write to the park superintendent at P. O. Box 279, Homestead, Florida 33030. Camping permits are free, but you must have one or you'll pay a stiff fine and may face eviction if someone else has reserved the site.

The Tennessee Valley Authority

The waterway system of the TVA is one of the East's great water-recreation areas. More than 600,000 acres of lakes, rivers, and reservoirs and 11,000 acres of shoreline set the scene for more than 200 campgrounds, 455 public-access areas, and public parks galore. Norris Lake alone has 800 miles of shoreline, three state parks, two state wildlife-management areas, and too many marinas, docks, resorts, and campsites to count.

The system is made up of cold mountain lakes as clear and remote as rain clouds, of brash white-water rivers, and of huge lakes such as Chickamauga and Nickajack. This is Daniel Boone country, drenched in history and still as rugged in some spots as it was when he hunted and fished these woods and waters.

Modern history is even more poignant because hundreds of farms and dozens of villages were covered by rising waters as dams and reservoirs replaced floodplains and streams. Fishermen with sophisticated depthsounders can see on their screens old roadbeds and bridge abutments that now lie at the bottoms of lakes. Along remote shores you'll stumble upon old cemeteries that were once at the edge of a village but are now many roadless miles from the people whose families are buried there.

Fishing is still the major magnet in the TVA lakes, though people also come for the hiking, ruby mining, wildlife photography, wildflower sketching, hunting, swimming, quaint mountain festivals, and, of course, boat camping. Locking through is part of the fun; it's free to recreational boats.

For information about the entire system ask for the booklet *Recreation on TVA Lakes* from TVA Information, 400 West Summit Hill Drive, Knoxville, Tennessee 37902 (615–254–7642).

Land Between the Lakes, in Kentucky and Tennessee, offers a marvelous variety of boat-camping pleasures. Camping is permitted almost anywhere on the seemingly endless shoreline. *Tennessee Valley Authority*

Land Between the Lakes, Kentucky and Tennessee

One of our favorite boat-camping haunts is the gorgeous Land Between the Lakes, a 170,000-acre, 40-mile-long playground peninsula between Lake Barkley and Kentucky Lake. Once you get away from the areas that can be reached by road, you leave the crowds far behind. Campsites are found throughout the Land Between the Lakes, but if you're willing to do without facilities, you can boat camp almost anywhere along the hundreds of miles of shoreline.

We've boat camped in the Land Between the Lakes for days without having to hobnob with other campers. After the extreme crowding we found at the developed campgrounds, it was like another world. Spring and fall offer the best weather and the

At The Homeplace–1850 in Land Between the Lakes interpretive characters go about their hosting and chores as though the twentieth century has not yet arrived. *Tennessee Valley Authority*

smallest crowds. Summertime offers the most activities—and they're good ones for the entire family.

We especially like The Homeplace–1850, a living-history farm where life goes on as it did in the mid-nineteenth century. An entire "family" works the farm all day, tending livestock, churning, kneading, quilting, spinning, splitting logs for fences, and stringing great lengths of "britches beans" to dry.

The family speak only in the parlance of the 1850s. It's great fun to spar with them verbally, asking where their sugar comes from (from New Orleans, by flatboat) or what they think of Henry Clay's slavery resolutions in Congress. Mention words like "radio" or "zipper," and you draw a blank. Throughout their workday these folks live in the pre–Civil War world.

One of the few drawbacks to LBL are its ticks. Be sure to take along a high-voltage tick repellent, not just a mosquito spray.

For information about boating and camping, contact Land Between the Lakes, 100 Van Morgan Drive, Golden Pond, Kentucky 42211 (502–924–5602).

Voyageurland, Minnesota

Boat camping the cold, clear lakes and pristine forests of northern Minnesota has been a way of life for as long as humankind has trod these shores. Indian history goes back for centuries, followed by waves of trappers, missionaries, lumberjacks, gold seekers, and finally today's travelers with their hunger for remote spots of exceptional beauty.

Scattered across Voyageurs National Park are more than 900 islands peppered with 300 individual campsites. Fish for northern pike or walleye. Watch for bald eagles and loons. Hike sun-dappled paths through towering forests. Go it completely alone, or try one of the resort packages that offer an overnight stay on an island.

Major lakes in the area include Clear Lake, Rainy Lake, and Moose Lake; rivers include the Rainy, Little Fork, Sturgeon, and Rat Root. Do your homework ahead of time, so you'll have an idea of what waterways are best for your kind of boating. Some are for canoes only; other areas have launch ramps for power craft.

When you arrive, look for current local information. Campsites may be closed temporarily because of bears, nesting eagles, erosion, or fire danger. Other campsites may be open but may forbid campfires because too much wood has been collected. You should gather only dead wood that's on the ground. Don't cut dead trees—they remain a habitat for wildlife. Where possible, use designated campsites. The sites were chosen for their environmental stability and for their ability to stand up under frequent usage. They are freer of bugs and have such equipment as bear-proof storage lockers, pit toilets, tent pads, and picnic tables.

For more information contact the Visitors and Convention Bureau, Box 169, International Falls, Minnesota 56649 (800–325–5766).

Boundary Waters Canoe Area, Minnesota and Ontario

One of America's greatest wildernesses, this unspoiled area is a heaven for canoeists. There's more lake than land, more woods and water than you can explore in a lifetime. Take your own equipment

Boat camping is permitted along the entire length of the Missouri River in South Dakota. *South Dakota Tourism*

or work with an outfitter who can supply a guide and gear for a week or two your family will always remember.

For information on the Superior National Forest and the Boundary Waters, call the Voyageur Visitor Center at 218–365–7681 or write to the Chamber of Commerce, 1600 East Sheridan Street, Ely, Minnesota 55731 (800–777–7281). Make your plans well in advance: permits are required for the Boundary Waters, and they're in heavy demand.

The Missouri River of South Dakota

Once called the Big Muddy because folks didn't know whether to plow it or drink it, the Missouri River meanders through the entire state of South Dakota from north to south. When the river was dammed it created a playland of clear, smooth-flowing waters that widen into massive lakes, locally called reservoirs or impoundments.

Amazingly, camping is available for the entire length of the river in South Dakota! You can start at the North Dakota border and follow the flow all the way to Nebraska and Iowa in what has to be one of the greatest boat adventures in America's heartland.

If you're canoeing, it's best to avoid the big impoundments, which can get windy and fractious, and concentrate on the area from Fort Randall Dam downstream to Gavins Point Dam and the naturally scenic old section of the river from Gavins Point Dam to Sioux City, Iowa.

Just keep in mind that lands immediately behind the public lands are privately owned, so don't trespass. Public areas, which extend from 100 yards to as much as a mile from the shoreline, are indicated by green and white markers.

For boats of all sizes, the river system offers hundreds of thousands of acres of water surface, some 3,000 miles of shoreline in the impoundments alone, and about 2,000 campsites in 40 developed recreation areas. Moreover, South Dakota looks out for its boat campers. After a storm, rangers check unattended campsites and vehicles; park officials also monitor marine radio.

Call South Dakota Tourism at 800–843–1930 for brochures on fishing, canoeing, and camping and for individual brochures on any or all of the four reservoirs: Lakes Oahe, Sharpe, Francis Case, and Lewis and Clark.

Kalispell and Environs, Montana

To "Morley" the magnificent waters of Montana means to "do" them in one of the museum-quality wood canoes made by Greg Morley. Exquisitely inlaid, the canoes are beautifully finished. What's more, they're excellent performers, favored by serious cruising canoeists. If you want to visit Morley's shop to talk about investing in your own canoe (for about $2,000), call 406–886–2242 for an appointment. Morley's work is also displayed at the Regional Craft House at Apgar.

No matter what boat you have, the mirrored lakes, awesome nature shows, and towering mountains of Glacier National Park are a stunning setting for boat camping. We counted eight campgrounds on the shores of Flathead Lake alone. You can also boat camp Whitefish Lake, Smith Lake, Little Bitterroot, and more.

For information, contact the Flathead Visitors Association, 15 Depot Loop, Kalispell, Montana 59901 (800–543–3105).

Canada

This enormous country has wonderful boat-camping areas. Many of them offer tame water and well-developed campgrounds. Others are so remote, cold, and challenging that they should be tackled only by well-equipped boat campers who are savvy about the ways of the North Country. Fortunately, many of the most difficult areas offer a wide choice of knowledgeable guides and outfitters. You don't have to go it alone, at least the first time.

For information, write to any or all of the following. From U.S. addresses, add Canada to the address and don't forget to affix the required postage!

- Alberta Tourism, 10025 Jasper Avenue, Edmonton, Alberta T5J 3Z3

- British Columbia Tourism, Parliament Building, Victoria, British Columbia V8V 1X4

- Manitoba Tourism, Department 9020, 155 Carlton Street, Winnipeg, Manitoba R3C 3H8

- New Brunswick Tourism, Box 12345, Fredericton, New Brunswick E3B 5C3

- Newfoundland/Labrador Tourism, Box 2016, St. John's, Newfoundland A1C 5R8

- Northwest Territories Tourism, Yellowknife, Northwest Territories X1A 2L9

- Nova Scotia Tourism, 136 Commercial Street, Portland, Maine 04101

- Ontario Tourism, Queens Park, Toronto, Ontario M7A 2E5

- Prince Edward Island Tourism, Box 940, Charlottetown, Prince Edward Island C1A 7M5

- Quebec Tourism, C.P. 20 000, Quebec, Quebec G1K 7X2

- Saskatchewan Tourism, 1919 Saskatchewan Drive, Regina, Saskatchewan S4P 3V7

- Yukon Tourism, Box 2703, Whitehorse, Yukon Territory Y1A 2C6

Kluane National Park, Yukon Territory

Long after the gold stampede of the 1890s was forgotten, visitors continued to be drawn to the Yukon by the dream of boat camping in the historic territory. The real "gold in them thar hills" is the sight of massive mountains second in size only to Mt. McKinley, the dazzling beauty of snow and ice, inky-blue lakes, prairie grasses and wildflowers, and frequent sightings of herds of wild animals. Boats can be launched on Kathleen Lake and outside the park on Kluane, Dezadeash, and Rainbow lakes.

Canoeing these waters is for experienced paddlers only. The 10-hour trip from Upper Rainbow Lake to west of Haines Junction has two half-hour-long portages and some stretches of Class III and Class IV rapids. The Dezadeash River also has a 28-mile-long canoe route. To spend a week in the backcountry, you can put in at Mush Lake and end up on Bates Lake, with a short portage in between.

For information, contact the Kluane National Park Reserve, Haines Junction, Yukon Territory YOB 1LO, Canada (403–634–2251).

Portland, Oregon

The Portland area is more beautiful than we could have imagined and not nearly as rainy as we'd been told. Boat-camping areas in the heart of the city include Sand Island Park, with its rich variety and abundance of waterfowl. A wildlife preserve across from St. Helens Marina, it's accessible only by boat. We also enjoy J. J. Collins Marine Park, another wildlife preserve, on Coon Island, that can be reached only by boat.

Boating and boat camping in this area are a feast of fishing, wildlife sightings, sunsets, waterfalls, and mountain shadows. You have your choice of the seacoast, the Columbia and Willamette rivers, and too many streams and lakes to mention.

For a free guide to access points, write to the Oregon State Marine Board, 3000 Market Street NE, Salem, Oregon 97310. Portland's tourism office can be reached at 800–962–3700.

Channel Islands National Park, California

Located in the wild Pacific Ocean off Ventura and Santa Barbara are the storybook islands of Anacapa, Santa Rosa, and San Miguel. They offer anchorages and camping—if you and your boat are up to the long, frisky crossing and an even friskier landing through savage surf. Anchoring is also permitted off a fourth island, Santa Cruz, but no landing is permitted without the advance permission of the landowners.

You can explore tide pools and grassy lowlands, watch for whales and porpoises, wander through ancient forests, and photograph elephant seals. But you must bring everything, including water, with you. It is high adventure and requires a sturdy boat and sturdy crewmembers, permits for camping and/or landing, and a great deal of planning. Call 805–644–8157 or write to the Ventura Visitors and Convention Bureau, 89–C South California Street, Ventura, California 93001 (805–648–2075).

Baja California

Baja is to the West Coast what the Bahamas are to eastern boaters: close, exotic, warm all year, and a boundless land of gunkholing paradises. Start by calling 800–44–MEXICO for very general information. Then visit your library to see what books, recent magazine articles, and newsletters are available on the area.

The Baja Explorer, a bimonthly magazine, is available from the ALTI Corporation, 4180 La Jolla Drive, La Jolla, California 92037.

3
Charting Your Course

If you have taken an authorized boating course as offered by the U.S. Coast Guard Auxiliary, the American Red Cross, or the U.S. Power Squadron, you already know basic piloting and navigation. If you haven't taken such a course, do so! Completing it will not only make you a more savvy skipper, it will probably qualify you for a price break on your marine insurance.

However, knowing how to find your way around the water is only half the battle in boat camping. You also need to know the lay of the land that surrounds you. For most boat-camping trips, we take a number of aids in addition to marine charts. Some of them may surprise you. The trick is to get enough charts and maps to find your way there and back without sinking your boat from the sheer weight.

Charts

For a free catalog that lists charts of American waters, write to the Distribution Branch (N/CG33), National Ocean Service, Riverdale, Maryland 20737. Charts of the following areas are available:

- The Atlantic and Gulf coasts, Puerto Rico, and the Virgin Islands
- The Pacific coast, Hawaii, Guam, and the Samoas
- Alaska, including the Aleutian Islands
- The Great Lakes and adjacent waterways
- Bathymetric/topographic and fishing maps

Within each of these areas are dozens of choices, ranging from large-scale planning charts to detailed charts of small areas. Once you have the catalog, you can order by credit card from 301–436–6990. If there is a National Ocean Service / National Oceanic and Atmospheric Administration (NOS/NOAA) chart dealer near you, you can also buy charts locally.

A superb source of NOS charts, as well as of British, Canadian, and French charts, is Bluewater Books, at 800–942–2583 (fax 305–522–2278; outside the United States, call 305–763–6533). Bluewater provides quick mail-order service anywhere in the world.

Charts of lakes and rivers are offered by the U.S. Army Corps of Engineers, 20 Massachusetts Avenue NW, Washington, DC 20314–1000.

In addition to charts, NOAA produces the U.S. Coast Pilot books. They provide weather and climate information, channel and anchorage information, and pilotage for specific coastal, intracoastal, and Great Lakes areas.

Light Lists are other publications that cover fog signals, radio-beacon characteristics, daymarkers, unlighted and lighted navigational aids, and Loran stations. They're more of interest to professional mariners. If you do buy one, for $15–$20, you'll have to update it from the weekly *Local Notice to Mariners*, which you can obtain free from the appropriate U.S. Coast Guard district office. Requests to be put on the mailing list must be made in writing to your district.

You can also keep your charts current through *Local Notice*. Charts themselves may be updated only every three or four years, so they can lag far behind in letting you know which buoys were swept away in spring floods or the location of the boat that sank recently and now constitutes an unseen hazard in your favorite harbor.

In tidal waters it's essential to have tide tables, which are available from NOS but are often found also in free fishermen's guides at tourism centers. The words "free" and "tourism center" are important, because so many maps, charts, and guides are available at no charge from sources that promote tourism. Some are not suitable for navigation, but all are worth looking at.

Maps and Other Guides

Every state and province has tourism-promotion agencies; they are a good place to start. Some even have toll-free numbers through which, with one call, you can unleash a torrent of

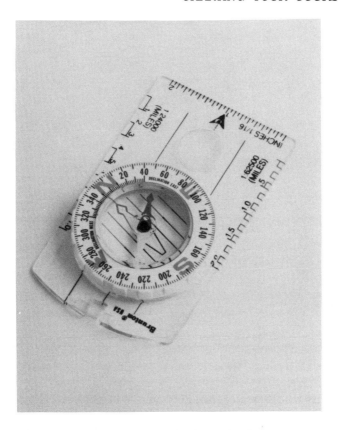

This Smoke Chaser compass, developed for the U.S. Forest Service to pinpoint forest fires, has luminous points for low-light use and is ideal for reading distances on topographic maps. *Brunton U.S.A.*

invaluable freebies. If you don't have an address and telephone number for the state, city, or region you want, a librarian can find it for you.

Begin by requesting a state map plus information on camping, boating, specific waterways, state parks, and fishing. At the same time, ask for brochures on any of your additional boat-camping interests such as wildflowers, rockhounding, or historic sites. Ask too for a list of city, county, and regional contacts through which you can obtain more specific information. Sometimes regional groups, especially those like Alabama's Mountain Lakes or the TVA,

Sometimes a non-marine compass is best for boat camping. Many specialty designs are available. *Brunton U.S.A.*

which focus on the water, are gold mines of boat-camping information.

Tourism-promotion groups often give away county or regional maps. Many of them are scrupulously correct and give excellent detail showing county and township roads that can take you from the water's edge to the nearest sightseeing or shopping. Others are not to scale or are so artsy they're worthless. So, start with the freebies and supplement them as necessary with proper maps and charts.

You can also find highly detailed street maps at chambers of commerce or in convention and visitor bureaus. They're invaluable when you're on foot in a community, such as Savannah or Charleston, in which the best sightseeing is within walking distance of the docks.

Among the most useful maps we have found are the Gazetteer books published by the DeLorme Mapping Company, Box 298, Freeport, Maine 40432 (800–227–1656 or 207–865–4171). Each book covers one state. Now available for about two dozen states, these books cover every road in the state, from the major highways to the smallest country lanes.

For serious hiking the best maps are topographical maps, called topo maps or simply topos for short. Start by getting a map index from the National Cartographic Information Center, 507 National Center, Reston, Virginia 22092. It will tell you what topos are available and where to order them. Shading, colors, and contour lines on topos provide volumes of insight into terrain characteristics. They give a complete picture of water and land, elevation and steepness, open spaces and forest, and the manmade environment, including dams, roads, and dwellings.

The reason for amassing these charts and maps is that as a boat camper you will be tied as firmly to the land as to the water. You're looking primarily for waterfront campsites, but you probably also want to seek out roads, rails, and trails and to avoid swamps, bogs, or heavily overgrown forests.

The best aid we've found to understanding maps, especially topographic maps, is a videotape, *The ABC's of Compass & Map,* available from Brunton U.S.A., 620 East Monroe Avenue, Riverton, Wyoming 82501 (307–856–6559). The 25-minute tape comes with a sophisticated little compass, an instruction book, and a workbook. For the boat-camping family, the video and sample exercises provide hours of winter pleasure while planning summertime cruises, camp-outs, and orienteering adventures.

One day you might venture away from the water to hike a historic trail along an abandoned railbed or an old canal towpath. The next day you might want to pick the shortest distance to a crossroads where you're likely to find a store selling outboard oil or fresh milk. Another time, you may be seeking medical help.

Without wheels, we've had wonderful adventures while looking for common conveniences: water, a telephone, hot showers, a supermarket, or a museum. As a break from camping, we occasionally stay in a cabin, resort, or bed-and-breakfast inn within walking distance of where we have docked or beached our boat.

Once, in the Florida Keys, the joke was on us. We found our way to U.S. 1 from the deserted dock where we had tied up and asked some passersby where the nearest coin-operated laundry was. We'd been gunkholing along Hawk Channel for two weeks without seeing a soul, and it was time for some serious suds.

Not realizing we didn't have a car, the strangers suggested cheerfully that we head north "for a few minutes" (at 60 mph). And, not realizing that the laundry was miles away, we started off with big sacks of dirty clothes on our backs. It was an all-day project, but we did make it there and back, all the time pondering the new world one sees when one is without wheels.

Many a river rat, out of gas along a deserted stretch of water, has had to find a road and hitchhike to the nearest gas station. With a good road map you can pinpoint the most likely places to find help: settlements, villages, crossroads, bridges. If you also have a CB radio, you can seek guidance from any motorist within talking range.

The land can also provide some of the richest finds in your trip: marked hiking paths, wildflower walks, wildlife sanctuaries, and nature exhibit centers. With highly detailed maps, we have found forgotten Civil War graves along the TVA system, ruins of once-baronial mansions along the New River, and ghost towns along Florida's St. Johns River and on Lake Michigan.

North America's early history was written along its coasts and waterways, well before a road system was established. To boat camp along rivers, canals, creeks, bayous, ocean beaches, and chains of lakes is to experience the very best in both boating and camping. And in most areas, from the impenetrable swamps of the Everglades to the roadless reaches of the Boundary Waters, to boat camp is to know the region in a privileged, intimate way available to no other type of visitor.

4

Know Where You Are, Keep in Touch

If you know where you are and have a means of communicating your location to others, all sorts of good things can happen—from being rescued in the nick of time to having a pizza delivered to your boat or campsite. Once, on a TVA lake, we listened to an agonizing exchange on an emergency channel. A guest on a boat had had a heart attack. The skipper sent a Mayday, and an ambulance was dispatched.

The problem was that the ambulance driver knew the roads but not the water, and the skipper knew the exact position of the boat on the lake but had no idea where it was in relation to the roads. Precious minutes ticked away as the dialogue went on and on.

As the drama played out we realized how little landlubbers know about the water and how sailors can be completely lost when it comes to logging roads, highways, hospitals, fire departments, the police, gas stations, and other land services that can suddenly become vital. Since that episode we've tried to carry the best road maps, as well as the best marine charts, when we go boat camping.

The Float Plan

Just as the filing of a flight plan is one of the pilot's most important safety tools, the float plan is the boat camper's best insurance policy. The more the authorities know about you, the description of your boat, and your intended route, the better the chances you'll be bailed out if you fail to show up at your checkpoints on time.

The purpose of a float plan is to assure (1) that someone will look for you even if you cannot radio or signal for help, (2) that they'll know what to look for, and (3) that they'll have an idea of where to start looking. It's a plus if they also have advance notice of any unusual circumstances they'll have to deal with when they find you—such as a handicapped child, a diabetic in insulin shock, or a person with a history of heart problems.

Use whatever float-plan form, camping permit, or other registration is suitable to the waterway or wilderness area you're entering. An additional precaution is to leave a detailed written itinerary with a friend or a relative. Most float-plan forms are terse and ask only for basic information, so it can be helpful if someone else knows that you're going to leave your "tan 1993 Blazer, license number ABC 1234, at the Meadow Point launch ramp on Tuesday morning at 7:00," that you'll "check in with Tom every evening at 8:00," or that you're "planning to meet Jim and Edie for dinner at the Rainbow Falls marina on Wednesday at 6:00 P.M."

In your detailed note you might also list some distinguishing features of your boat and your camping gear—such as "Our tent is green and has a matching screen room" or "We have two red ice chests with white lids"—the names and addresses of the people who are with you, and any medical information that rescuers should know, such as "Jenny is four months pregnant" or "Ralph is diabetic and is leaving port on May 28th with a six-day supply of insulin."

We live in an area where boating is a year-round passion, so almost every day we hear of a happy ending to a rescue that was made possible by the joint efforts of the boater, the authorities, and well-informed friends or relatives at home.

The Weather Report

Experienced campers learn to sense a change in the weather through the winds and the sky, the turning of leaves, and even bird calls. The more you tune in to nature, the more eloquent a story you can hear. That's where boating adds an exciting plus to the weather-forecasting skills of the camper.

You can see the sky more clearly and sense the wind direction more accurately on water than on land. The water itself is often the first telltale, its mirror surface crinkling into cat's-paws and the cat's-paws kicking up into something sloppier. As both boater and

FLOAT PLAN

Phone Numbers

Coast Guard: _____

Local Marine Police: _____

Description of the Boat

Boat Name: _____ Type: _____

Hailing Port: _____

Make: _____ Length: _____ Beam: _____ Draft: _____

Color, Hull: _____ Cabin: _____ Deck: _____ Trim: _____ Dodger: _____

Distinguishing Features: _____

Registration No: _____ Sail No: _____

Engine(s) Type: _____ Horsepower: _____ Cruising Speed: _____

Electronics/Safety Equipment Aboard

VHF Radio: _____ DB: _____ SSB: _____ Loran: _____ SatNav: _____

Depthsounder: _____ Radar: _____ EPIRB: _____ Other: _____

Raft: _____ Dinghy: _____

Trip Details

Name of Person Filing Report: _____

Phone: _____

Additional Persons Aboard, Total: _____

Name: _____ Age: _____

Phone: _____

Name: _____ Age: _____

Phone: _____

Name: _____ Age: _____

Phone: _____

Name: _____ Age: _____

Phone: _____

Departure

Date/Time: _____ Return No Later Than: _____

Depart From: _____

Fuel Aboard (Quantity): _____ Estimated Cruising Range: _____

Marina (Home Port)

_____

Phone: _____

Destination Port

_____

ETA: _____ No Later Than: _____

Phone: _____

Anticipated Stopover Ports

_____

ETA: _____ No Later Than: _____

Phone: _____

_____

ETA: _____ No Later Than: _____

Phone: _____

_____

ETA: _____ No Later Than: _____

Phone: _____

Plan Filed With

Name: _____

Phone: _____

Towing Company: _____

Phone: _____

Remarks

_____

_____

_____

_____

_____

_____

camper, you can be a far better meteorologist than can the land-locked camper or the seagoing sailor alone.

If you have a VHF radio, you can hear about weather on channel 22A. If you don't, find any portable radio that is capable of picking up NOAA (WX–1, WX–2, WX–3) weather radio or one of the Coast Guard marine information stations. Some sets, including automobile radios and portables, have an "alert" feature that turns them on automatically when a weather emergency is broadcast.

Communications Radios

The marine communications radio of choice is the VHF, and the classic communications radio on land has long been the CB. The boat camper can use either or both, plus such exciting new devices as pagers and cellular telephones. So important have cell phones become on the highway, in fact, that truckers' CB channels are increasingly quiet.

Both pagers and cell phones have become more powerful, commonplace, and affordable. They can be used by most boat campers most of the time, and their influence continues to spread. Factors that limit their use include your budget, the availability of power, and how much you really want to bother with the outside world.

For marine communications, VHF is indispensable for talking to other boats, bridgetenders, lockkeepers, marinas, the Coast Guard, or other emergency services and for making reservations at waterfront restaurants. VHF radio can transmit only about as far as you can see, plus a little bonus for the height of the antennas. At most, you can probably talk to people who are within 20 miles of your radio. Hand-held and built-in models are available.

Rules for using your VHF are enforced by the Federal Communications Commission. Failure to comply could result in a warning, a citation, loss of your license, fines of up to $500 per day, and/or a jail term.

For details on how to order the *Marine Radiotelephone Users Handbook,* write to the Radio Technical Commission for Marine Services, Federal Communications Commission, P. O. Box 19087, Washington, DC 20036. Also available is a handbook of safety-information sources, which lists data bases, radio broadcasts, and publications that are available to keep you current on navigation aids in your cruising area.

No license is needed to operate a CB radio, which usually works within a range of about five miles. A CB isn't a substitute for a VHF in marine emergencies, although some services do monitor channel 9, the CB emergency channel.

In some island groups and waterways CBs are used more commonly than VHFs. For boat campers an added advantage of a CB is that it's sometimes more important to communicate with a passing trucker, a nearby RV, or a "Smokey" than with another boat. Keep in mind that although you don't need a license to use a CB, any work on the radio unit must be done by a licensed professional.

Amateur or ham radio doesn't interest most boat campers because it requires so much equipment, power, and extensive training. However, amateur radio is one of the most useful and educational of all family hobbies, and most dedicated hams will find a way to take a rig along on a boat-camping trip.

If you have what it takes to get the gear and the licenses, ham radio can provide hours of fun as well as crucial communications during emergencies. After Hurricane Hugo devastated the Virgin Islands, hams on shore and in the live-aboard fleet were the islands' only link with the outside world. To learn how to get started in amateur radio, write to the American Radio Relay League, Newington, Connecticut 06111.

Other Means of Communication

Traditions of the sea include other forms of communication, such as flag hoists and semaphore signals, but we think they're a waste of time except in very yachty communities or in international coastal areas. Sad to say, flag etiquette and other old formalities are becoming lost arts. Besides, most boat campers don't have room to carry an entire suit of signal flags and pennants.

One time-honored system that is still worth learning is the Morse code. If you can capture the interest of children in the "secret-code" stage—when they're about 8 to 10 years old—you can provide a skill that can be used throughout life.

The Morse code can be practiced on long, boring passages or drives and, after lights-out, by two or more people or by one person alone. It's simply a matter of tapping a finger on an imaginary key.

A child who is "grounded" as punishment really thinks he's getting away with something if he can tap out messages to the other kids with a couple of sticks. Meanwhile, they're all honing an important skill.

The code can be used visually, with a flashlight or a blinker, or audibly, with a buzzer, a radio, a bass drum, a whistle, or any other device that will broadcast your message.

A bullhorn, more commonly called a hailer or a loud hailer in boating, can also be a useful communications tool in docking, retrieving, hitching, launching, locking, and rescuing. Hand-held units are available: we have one that is built into the CB. Like other noisemakers, though, a hailer is an intrusion that most of us like to avoid.

Air horns are even more unpleasant to listen to, but you may need one to signal bridgetenders. The sound carries for miles, so it's useful in some emergency situations, too.

An Emergency Position Indicating Radio Beacon (EPIRB) sends a signal from the water to airplanes. It's the seagoing counterpart of the Emergency Location Transmitter (ELT) used in aircraft. The chief difference is that in an airplane crash the ELT begins to transmit automatically; the EPIRB is best deployed in the water, and it may be automatic or may have to be switched on manually. EPIRBs are expensive and are of more interest to blue-water sailors who aren't likely to have other means of calling for help.

Signal flares, which are required on many boats, are important to the boat-camper's rescue vocabulary. They are discussed in Chapter 10.

Navigation Aids

Although highly sophisticated electronic navigation devices are now small enough and affordable enough for small-boat use, our guess is that few boat campers will have Loran, radar, or GPS on board. The more savvy you are about navigation and the more electronic help you have, the better. However, in river and coastal cruising there's no substitute for good pilotage. What you can see with your eyes—markers, charts, buoys, landmarks—is usually more impor- tant than what you try to see, think you see, or hope to see in a flickering LCD display. The closer you are to land, traffic, and other hazards, the more important vigilance becomes.

We once answered a Mayday call from a sailor who was lost between Porgee Rock (the last landmark in New Providence) and Highbourne Cay, a crossing of less than 30 miles. He was trying to find his position by taking sun sights with his sextant! Land was within sight for almost the entire crossing, and all the lost sailor needed to do was to climb halfway up the mast with his binoculars and look around.

Today's electronic aids make navigation easy. Newer technologies are accurate to within a few feet. To depend on these devices instead of on constant lookout and on keeping track of your position on a chart, however, is to ask for trouble. The smaller and more crowded the waterway, the easier and more important eyeball navigation becomes.

The one electronic device that is most common in boat camping is the depthsounder/fish-finder—a must for fishermen but also a very useful navigation aid. The most sophisticated units paint such a clear picture of the bottom that you can spot a single fish.

If we could only have one electronic aid aboard, it would be a depthsounder. In navigation you can tell a great deal about where you are by the depth of the water. A depthsounder can help you find an anchorage that is free of snags and to avoid hazards of all kinds.

We're told that the great storms on Lake Erie can alter the bottom profile tremendously from one season to another. A good depthsounder can warn you of new hazards that weren't there last year. In Florida Bay, huge blocks of granite recently jettisoned from a distressed ship can be avoided. In the Thousand Islands of the St. Lawrence River, a depthsounder helped us pick our way through deep channels in which some rocks rose almost to the surface.

The one other navigation aid you might consider carrying is a Radio Direction Finder. A small, portable, battery-operated unit can double as an entertainment radio. In navigation it can point the way to the nearest station, including commercial radio stations, or to two stations from which you can triangulate your exact position.

II
The Equipment

5
Fitting Out Your Boat

How small is small? How rough can the water get? How much can you and/or the boat take?

Each boat camper will have his or her own answers to these questions, but your small boat *can* be modified for longer, riskier adventures or to carry more gear than it was designed for.

Strengthening Your Boat

Three days off San Salvador, Bahamas, we lay ahull all night in 20-foot Atlantic seas in a 29-foot boat, trusting that it could take more than we could. It could! On the other hand, we once refused a magazine assignment in a 22-foot twin outboard we were to take across Lake Huron on a gusty day. Soon after we turned the boat over to another writer, it came apart at the garboard.

The point is that volumes can be written about how to make a boat stronger and more seaworthy, but it all boils down to (1) the total integrity of the boat, including any modifications you have made; (2) your ability to pilot and navigate within the limits of the boat, and the day's weather and water conditions; and (3) luck.

We know what it is to go 75 mph in a bass boat, to boil through Class V rapids, to skim swamps in an airboat, to sail rail down in a rollicking ocean, to float at walking speed down a Florida spring "run," and to go zero mph in a canoe against high winds and chop. Every kind of boating has its own pleasures and terrors.

Small can be beautiful. While sailing the Bahamas we met a young family who were boat camping the islands in a Boston whaler. It was the adventure of a lifetime and, with their speedy outboard, they saw more of the islands in two weeks than we did in a month. Another family, with a 4-year-old daughter, were sailing the islands in a 22-foot sloop.

A growing number of people want bigger action from smaller boats. They are demanding quality, durability, flotation, and safety in boats of all kinds, not just in big blue-water yachts. Fortunately, the marine industry is answering their call for better boats in smaller sizes, and today buyers have a wide choice of great boats at realistic prices.

Dos and Don'ts

Now that you have the boat, are there things you can do to give you that extra mile?

Things not to do, of course, include overloading, overpowering, overpropping, overstressing, or breaking any of the other laws and rules that have been worked out by the manufacturer's expert engineers, the U.S. Coast Guard, and marine industry standard setters.

Every boat has a label that tells how many people, how many pounds, and how many horses it is rated for. Read the owner's manual, too. From it you'll learn what the boat can and can't do.

For example, most of us think it would be a blast to pull the lanyard on a liferaft at a party, just as we've seen on TV. However, the owner's manual will tell you that this could ruin the raft. It was designed to handle certain stresses and temperatures only when it's supported by water. If you blow it up for fun or practice, it could rip from the stress or crack from the shock of the cold gases that suddenly invade its warm fabric.

By reading the manual of another boat you'll learn that it requires a certain trailer-bed design to support specified parts of the hull when it's out of the water. The farther you trail the boat, the more important it is to give it the best support on the trailer. The same can be said of hauling or stacking techniques. Supports must be placed correctly to protect the hull.

A common source of trouble is a bow cleat that was not intended to be used to tow the boat off a sandbar, or a towing ring that was not designed for steep or difficult ramps. Serious injuries have resulted when a fastener broke loose and was catapulted into someone's noggin by a well-stretched nylon line—all because somebody expected more of the fitting than the manufacturer intended.

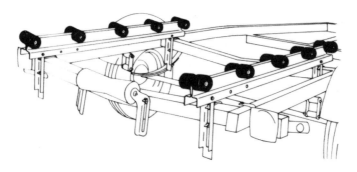

Read your owner's manual to learn what supports your boat needs when it's on its trailer. Stresses are different when a boat is out of the water. *Dutton–Lainson*

Your first step should be to contact the manufacturer to see if there have been any recalls or reinforcements since your boat was built. You may not have heard about serious defects, especially if you're not the original owner.

Call the U.S. Coast Guard Boating Safety Hotline at 800–368–5647 and ask whether your model of boat has any known potential safety defects. It's a two-way information line, to which you can report safety problems with your boat. The Coast Guard keeps track of such reports and investigates them, then calls for corrections or recalls if necessary.

Contact owners of boats, engines, sails, and other gear like yours to ask about their experiences with worst-case situations. Many brands have owners' clubs, which are gold mines of information.

Every part of every boat will fail at some point, so you're ahead of the game if you know that the transoms of Boat A are subject to dry rot, that the welds that hold the seats to the hull in Boat B are subject to shearing after a year or two, or that Boat C is famous for developing osmotic blisters.

If your boat is an orphan, try publishing letters to the editor in boating magazines, asking to hear from owners of similar boats. Exchange information. Network.

Once you're familiar with what the boat was designed to do and not to do and with how well it has performed in the field, there are some modifications that you can make.

If your boat is aluminum and you pull up on shore each night to make camp, the hull will soon be scoured thin. Ask the manufacturer about the availability of a protective shoe that can be put on the hull to keep it from being ground away by repeated beachings. If none is available, consider adding a sacrificial layer of fiberglass.

In his book *Arctic Passages* John Bockstoce explains how he reinforced the 20-foot freighter canoe, a traditional cedar-and-canvas craft, he used in Alaska. Heavy layers of fiberglass were added around the places in the bow and stern that would be bashed by ice. He also added oak runners parallel to the keel to prevent wearing of the hull when the canoe was hauled up on rocky shores. Inside the canoe Bockstoce installed a two-by-four-inch keelson and put four vertical two-by-twos between the keelson and the thwarts to prevent the bottom from flexing when rough seas pounded it.

In addition to strengthening the hull, you can get better ground tackle. Boat camping is serious, overnight cruising that will take you through a variety of waters and bottoms. We carry a small folding anchor, even in the smallest boat on the shortest outing. It's useful as a "lunch hook" and for holding the stern off a beach if we want to tie the bow ashore. For overnight anchoring, we like to have at least two types of hooks—where one won't bite, the other will. It won't hurt to go a bit oversize on the anchor(s) and on the rode(s).

Even if you never intend to anchor out, ground tackle is important because a hook is the only brake your boat will have in all sorts of emergencies. It's also a wise precaution to run an anchor well inland when the boat is completely beached, so that a rising tide or an immense wake from a passing boat can't float your craft and take it away. We once met a man who had boat camped his way down the Mississippi River in a john boat. He found that the wakes from passing towboats went on all night—and were formidable.

Add backing plates where necessary. If deck fittings have been mounted through thin hull or deck material, when they are over-stressed they can pull out and take a big chunk of the boat with them. Consider adding backing plates inside the hull under winches, downriggers, cleats, oarlocks, and where other fittings are attached to the boat.

The towing eye that is used to launch and retrieve the boat may be adequate for a lightly loaded boat on a good ramp. A stronger eye, with a better backing plate, will give you a margin of safety when the boat is heavily loaded and the ramp is steep or rough. Eyes are available with very long bolts; a V-block can be added for extra strength.

Reinforce the hull–deck joint. It's another weak spot / leak spot on many boats. Check yours out for adequate fastenings and for thorough bedding. The hull–keel joint can also be a trouble spot, especially in one of the new boats with a releasable keel.

Robert Manry added polyurethane foam to his *Tinkerbelle* for more flotation and a heavy weight to its daggerboard keel so that it would right itself even if it rolled on its beam ends. For design changes like these it's best to seek the advice of a marine architect.

If you'll be docking and/or locking often, you may need larger cleats than are provided on many boats. Also, the sides of the hull will take a great deal of extra punishment in locks. Rubrails are called that for good reason! Some are little more than cosmetic, so if yours are flimsy, consider replacing them with two-part rails with a replaceable filler. Some take nylon cordage in standard sizes, which is easy and inexpensive to replace when it's ragged or grubby. At resale time, a bright new rubrail can give the boat a whole new look. By installing the refillable rails now, you can replace the filler as often as you like.

You may need more fuel and water tankage. Because gasoline

weighs six pounds per gallon and water eight pounds per gallon, considerable thought has to go into placement of these tanks.

Ready-made lay-up covers aren't usually designed to do the same thing, or to take the same punishment, as the enclosure you'll be putting up each night to turn your boat into a shelter. Get a better design, in a heavier-duty material, with stronger fittings. Incorporate windows or vents for sleeping comfort. For serious boat camping, it will pay to have a proper cover custom-made by a professional.

Removable covers, such as Bimini tops, dodgers, and spray shields, can allow you to tolerate sea, splash, sun, or wind conditions that aren't a problem to the boat but are a problem to its crew. It's best to have them custom-made by professionals, using materials that will stand up to wet, stress, and ultraviolet rays.

Although it's tempting to double up here and to reinforce there, we suggest that you don't go—pardon the pun—overboard. Some components are designed to flex. By reinforcing them and making them rigid, you might make things worse. A common mistake, especially for backyard boatbuilders at work on their first boat, is to figure that if four layers of mat and roving are good, eight layers will be twice as good, or that if 1/4-inch plywood is called for in the plans, 3/8 is better.

We've seen some homemade boats that were so ponderous they couldn't get out of their own way. One good punch from a piling and they were holed or splintered. Yet we've seen paper-thin hulls bash in and pop right back out again as though nothing had happened.

Heavier rigging or a thicker mast can change the boat's weight and balance. Any additions above the waterline will also increase drag, which can make a sailboat markedly slower and a powerboat both slower and less fuel efficient. Additions below the waterline weigh little when the boat is in the water, but they too can increase drag by adding weight or by distorting the original lines. And they add to the total weight you're hauling on the trailer, on top of your car, and in portages.

Adding to your boat doesn't necessarily mean adding thickness and weight. Engineering and common sense are the key.

Stowage Areas

Adding or modifying storage areas will probably be a must in any guppy-sized boat you'll be using for whale-sized cruising. Before calling in a ship's carpenter, think things through. A common

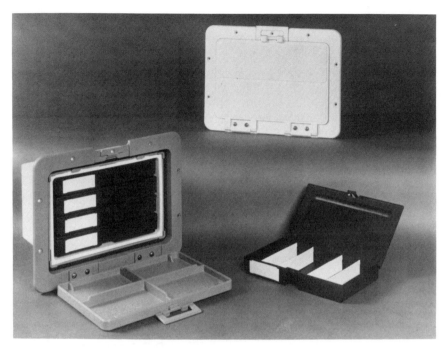

Stowage modules that come complete with hatch and flange are available in marine–supply stores. Simply cut a hole in the deck or a bulkhead, drop in the module after bedding thoroughly, and screw it in. You'll have a new compartment that looks as though it were factory installed. Modules come in various sizes and configurations. *Tempress*

mistake made by people who have small boats is to fit in all the comforts of home, including galley and head, in such dollhouse miniature that they won't work for people of normal size. In boat camping it's usually better to have a portable head and portable galley because you can set them up at the campsite, in the cockpit, or wherever is best for each day. With built-ins, you're stuck with one layout.

Some of the best additions cost little and can be done by anyone. Hang stowage hammocks from brass cup hooks. Install self-adhesive Velcro hooks and straps. Stick up self-adhesive hooks to hold light items, such as pot holders or dish towels.

Create stowage spaces for charts or bottles by lining a locker with lengths of thin-wall PVC pipe. Install fittings to which you can attach straps or bungee cords in several configurations to anchor oversized or odd-shaped gear. Consider adding furring strips to keep heavy items, such as the portable toilet or the ice chest, from sliding around when you're under way.

Improving Your Gear

Footwear is probably the one apparel item that differs most in boating and in camping. Boaters want shoes that are lightweight, flexible, and nonskid. Campers want sturdy hiking boots that support the feet and ankles while taking plenty of punishment: harsh wear, soaking, scrambling around all sorts of surfaces from sand to shale, and even snakebite. Footwear can range from the mere bootees worn by canoers to the snakeproof, calf-high clodhoppers worn by hikers and climbers.

Is there a compromise? One answer for those who want more than boat shoes and less than hiking boots is to waterproof leather boat shoes with a product such as Sno-Seal, a beeswax coating that dries solid and stays on the surface of the leather, keeping water out while allowing the foot to breathe. Silicone products, by contrast, migrate through leather and eventually clog the pores, keeping water out but also keeping perspiration in.

Also available in outdoor supply stores is Welt-Seal, a rubber adhesive that seals stitching and seams in footwear. It can also be used to seal seams in tents, inflatable boats, rainwear, and other boating and camping gear.

Silicone Water-Guard is available in a dauber kit or as a spray. It can waterproof—or increase waterproofing on—clothing, tents, sleeping bags, and the like. Sold in camping-supply stores, it is 10 percent silicone, compared with the 2–5 percent silicone contained in most popular supermarket brands.

Waterproofing is the most important addition to gear you will use in serious boat camping. Day sailors and weekenders can put up with wet and damp for the short term. When you're on a cruise of a week or more, however, wetness becomes more than mere discomfort. Mildew leaves ugly stains. Rot begins to destroy wood and fabric. Bad smells waft from dank gear. Skin problems begin. It's said that during World War I more soldiers were felled by trench foot than by bullets. Dry feet aren't a luxury, they're a boat-camping necessity.

Probably the second most important item to add to your equipment is sun covers, sail bags, and stuff bags. Almost everything you buy these days, from sleeping bags to camp stoves, comes in a storage bag that's worthless. Yet most of these covers and bags are crucial. They keep sails from rotting, stoves from being banged up, flashlights and lanterns from being smashed, sleeping bags from being soaked, and loose gear from floating over the side.

Where possible, buy the best available cover, protector, or sack offered by the original manufacturer. It will probably be the best fabric and fit for the job. Coleman, for example, makes a lantern which comes in a plastic container that could probably go over Niagara Falls without damage.

Sometimes you can find the right stowage box or bag in a ready-made item. Canvas ice bags, for example, are a classic choice for carrying and corralling miscellaneous gear. In other cases you'll have to make or have made good covers using the right fabrics with the right fasteners or drawstrings for rugged service.

6

Canvas Capers

Boat camping is as old as birchbark, but as technology continues to merge with human ingenuity, variations on the theme continue to grow. The variations almost always involve some combination of boat and fabric that results in maximum shelter in minimum hull size: sailboats with pop-up cabin tops, pontoon boats with full or partial fabric enclosures, and foldaway cockpit enclosures with screened windows.

Home Is Where the Tarp Is

Your boat-camping life will involve one or all of the following:

- You'll always sleep on the boat, at anchor or at dockside
- You'll sleep afloat or ashore, depending on conditions, using the boat as all or part of a shelter
- You'll always sleep ashore

Sleeping Aboard the Boat

We cruised the entire length of the Trent–Severn Waterway in a 22-foot twin outboard boat that had a tiny enclosed cabin outfitted with two bunks and a portable toilet. We slept on board at anchor or at marinas.

The galley was portable and was set up on the deck, the dock, or the beach, according to conditions. A canvas cockpit enclosure gave us additional space for bathing, dressing, and meal preparation on

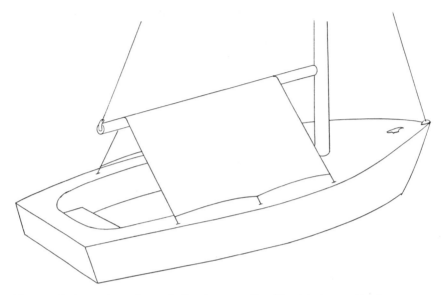

The simplest way to make a shelter in a small sailboat is to use the boom as a ridgepole. Snaps can be put on the boat and in the cover to add additional canvas fore and aft. *Gordon Groene*

rainy days. Although the boat was small, it was too deep and heavy to be run up on the beach. We had to anchor or dock.

You'll probably be sleeping afloat if you have a boat with big outboard or I/O (inboard-outboard) engines or a sailboat with a single keel. You may have to sleep afloat, even in the tiniest boat, along some bayous and hammocks where banks are too boggy to make camp, in river canyons surrounded by sheer cliffs, and in the lee of rocky islands that offer no landing place. We've spent many blissfully bug-free nights sleeping afloat on the Bahama Banks, miles from the nearest land, in water only 8 or 10 feet deep.

Sleeping Ashore or Afloat

Perhaps your boat is small and shallow-draft enough to be run up on the beach, giving you the option of sleeping on shore when you choose to. Examples include a catamaran with a tent enclosure over the trampoline; inflatable boats; twin-keel sailboats that settle comfortably into the bottom as the tide goes out, or a trailerable boat

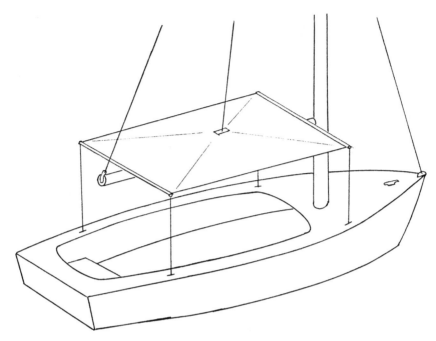

One way to enclose a small sailboat is to use a flat tarp that is strengthened on each end with battens and held up by the topping lift. It can be fitted with curtains on all four sides. If you have a small hole made in the middle, it can be fitted with an adapter that takes a piece of vinyl tubing. Run the tubing into a water jug. Drop the topping lift until the top is concave instead of convex, and you have an effective water catchment. *Gordon Groene*

that can be retrieved from the water, set up in a campsite, and used as an RV.

Making Camp Ashore Nightly

When your boat is too small to provide living comforts, you make camp on the beach nightly, using tents and other equipment you carry on the boat and off-load. Examples include racing catamarans, smaller inflatables, canoes or kayaks, john boats or skiffs, and the smallest pontoon boats.

Variations on this theme include using camping shelters instead of a tent. You'll find KOA campgrounds that have Kamping Kabins,

You can fold a well-made Bimini top completely away when you want an open boat. By day the top provides protection from the sun. Fitted with side curtains, by night it can turn the cockpit into a snug, dry sleeping area. *Westland Boat Covers & Tops*

which are bunkhouses with no other facilities. Other KOAs also provide Kamping Kitchens, so you won't need to bring cooking equipment.

In some Everglades campgrounds "chickee" shelters are available. You'll need only a sleeping bag and mosquito netting, plus cooking gear. At Burton Island State Park in Lake Champlain, your campsite comes with a lean-to. You bring in all your other gear, but you don't need a tent.

What Kinds of Canvas?

Many years ago, when both pontoon boats and pop-top camper trailers were fairly uncommon, we met a family in the TVA lakes who had combined the two. Starting with a basic, no-frills pontoon platform boat, they bought a pop-out camper for almost nothing because its undercarriage was shot. The camper itself, with a double bed in each of its two foldout wings, was still in good condition.

These folks simply mounted the camper atop the pontoon deck on a platform that raised the camper high enough so that when its wings were opened they would clear the rails. The boxy platform formed a cavernous stowage compartment for all the bedding and gear. Mom and Pop slept on one side, the kids on the other, and a portable potty occupied the middle section. They cruised the lakes, content as clams.

The previous owner of the little sloop that was our home for 10 years had equipped it with some of the most clever canvas shelters we've ever seen. The cockpit was shaded by a square of waterproof fabric that was held up by a halyard attached to its center and was stiffened by battens fore and aft. Grommets at the corners allowed further tying down.

Three waterproof fabric "walls" could be attached to this top with brass fittings. With all three "walls" in place, the enclosure turned the cockpit into a "room" that was almost completely weatherproof.

If we just wanted shading from low sun, we could attach only one or two of the "walls." If we wanted to form a water catch, we could lower the halyard until the top formed a cup instead of a peak. We then attached a piece of vinyl tubing to a fitting in the center and put the other end in a jerry jug.

A folding wooden framework could be put up over a forward hatch and covered with another canvas cover. This one had zippered, screened "windows" on all four sides. When everything was closed up it formed a small, leakproof space that allowed a bit of headroom in the tiny forepeak. When only the windward "window" was unzipped, it formed a wind scoop.

Under way, the whole system folded away to take up no more space than a sail. Stripped, our sailboat was as lean and mean as the day it was launched. Yet fully festooned at anchor it sprouted another foot of headroom forward and an enclosed cockpit that could sleep two children.

In boat camping, fabrics can be used to provide protection from sun, rain, and wind, can be rigged to direct cooling breezes where they are needed, and can fold away and disappear during the day.

Selecting Fabrics

Unless you're an experienced canvas worker with a good source of marine-quality supplies, it's best to have custom covers made by a professional who knows the marine scene. Fabrics come in many weights, from silky films to heavy-as-hide. Coatings too can be water resistant or water-tight, with or without good resistance to damage from harsh sun, mildew, abrasion, and repeated soakings. The best compromise must be found: a fabric light enough to be portable and heavy enough to take whatever stresses it is intended for. It must be as waterproof as necessary for this use and as tightly woven as necessary to provide the sun protection you need.

Your project will probably involve one or more of the following fabrics:

Vinyl-coated Dacron. Known by such trade names as Boat Top, this is one of the most durable and waterproof fabrics afloat, so it's a good choice for cockpit enclosures and awnings. Because it's waterproof, however, it also allows condensation to collect inside the enclosure as you sleep. Unless you provide good ventilation, you may wake up in the morning to the pitter patter of "rain" on your face. The precipitation comes not from the sky but from your shelter's ceiling.

Mosquito netting. Strong nylon netting can be sewn into your cockpit cover to give you ventilation. Make sure you get the finest mesh available to prevent no-see-ums from flying through, and flaps that can be closed when it rains.

Clear vinyl. Make sure to buy heavy-duty see-through vinyl with good optical qualities. Putting windows in your cockpit enclosure will add to the cost and complexity (for privacy you'll need a flap over each window), but the windows will pay for themselves on the first rainy day you're stuck inside. You'll be able to see what's going on outside, and you'll welcome the light the window provides.

Solution-dyed acrylic. Tough and water resistant, fabrics known by such names as Sunbrella withstand fading and mildew. They aren't waterproof, which means they breathe and are less apt to allow condensate to collect.

Ultraviolet-coated Dacron. Available in various weights, these light fabrics provide the best sun protection. At five ounces or less per yard, they are a good choice to make into sun flies. Simply hem a piece of the material in any size you want and put grommets at all four corners and, especially for larger flies, at intervals along the edges. You can then rig sunshades anywhere ashore or afloat, depending on what trees or rigging are available to tie them onto.

A professional may also have access to fittings you can't buy in ordinary fabric shops. It pays to invest in the best brass, nylon, or stainless-steel fasteners, heavy-duty plastic or brass zippers, heavy-duty vinyl "window" materials, screens that can take lots of punishment, coated threads, and the best seam waterproofers. One source of these specialized materials is the Sailrite *Sailmaker's Catalog*, 305 West Van Buren Street, Columbia City, Indiana 46725 (800–348–2769). If you're an avid sewer and want to tackle your own canvas work, we recommend Jim Grant's *The Complete Canvasworker's Guide* (International Marine).

About Tents

"Choose your first tent as if it were your last," advises Ken Kearns of Eureka! Tents. "Even bad tents can look nice initially, so it's possible to leave a store with what you think is a nice little starter tent. What you really have is a nightmare." Kearns suggests four guidelines.

1. Look for dryness. Often it isn't the rain that makes you wet, it's your body. "Each body gives off about a pint of water during the night," Kearns explains. "If your tent doesn't have good ventilation, moist air has no way of getting out. It condenses on the tent's roof and walls. A cheap tent will get you wet whether it rains or not."

According to Kearns, a tent should have a breathable roof, a waterproof fly, and hooded doors and windows, which guarantee good ventilation even in hard rains. "Look at the seams where the walls meet the floor," he suggests. "Better-quality tents have heavy-duty polyurethane-coated floors that wrap up the walls to eliminate seams at ground level."

2. Look for durability. Cheaper tents fail first at stress points, such as corners, frame-attachment points, doors, windows, roof peaks, and floor seams. A good tent will be reinforced in these areas, especially where the frame meets the floor. The best frames, Kearns believes, are those made of aluminum alloy or fiberglass. He likes a frame with shock-cord suspension, which acts as a shock absorber during heavy winds and when people are moving around inside the tent. This eliminates stress on both the frame and the fabric.

3. Look for easy setup. Again, Kearns likes shock-cord that runs the length of each frame to keep the pieces together. Pieces can't be lost or confused. If the shock-cords have clip attachments, setup will be quicker and more hassle free. "Practice setting up the tent first at home. This is also a good time to seal the seams," he suggests.

4. Buy a bigger tent than you think you need, allowing room for gear and not just for the people who will be sleeping in it. This is an individual decision, and it will depend on how much tent you can find room for in your own boat. The Eureka! Chateau cabin tent, 11′9″ by 8′9″, weighs 29 pounds. The compact Timberline, 4′6″ by

Caring for a Nylon Tent

Here, from the tent experts at the Coleman Company, are the steps to take in preparing and using your new nylon tent.

1. Lay the tent out flat and use two even coats of seam sealer in needle holes inside and out. Read the manufacturer's directions. Roof seams may need to breathe, so sealing may not be recommended.

2. Pick a tent site that is free of sharp sticks and stones and of depressions in which water might collect, and spread out a ground cloth that is slightly smaller than the tent floor. If the cloth extends beyond the tent, it will funnel water under the tent.

3. Use special tent stakes in special situations. Sand stakes hold better in loose sand; steel stakes, in soil that is rocky, hard, or frozen. Skewer stakes have more holding power with less weight.

4. Unless the manufacturer's directions indicate machine washing, clean tents only with a sponge and mild soap.

5. Lubricate zippers regularly with silicone, especially in sandy areas where grit abrades the teeth. Don't force a stuck zipper.

6. Store a tent dry, loosely folded, and away from heat. Don't store a tent directly on a concrete floor. Be generous with mouse bait around the house and storage areas: mice like to nest in tents and can gnaw holes in them.

7. If repairs are needed, use the tape or repair material recommended by the tent manufacturer.

8. Never operate any fuel-burning device inside a tent! Oxygen is consumed, and carbon monoxide is formed.

7'8" with 3'6" of headroom, weighs less than five pounds. And the Eureka! Gossamer, just big enough to shelter one person, weighs less than three pounds.

"Don't overlook optional accessories such as vestibules and gear lofts," Kearns adds. An alternative to getting a larger tent is to get a separate screen house for cooking and eating.

Not all screen rooms are the same. Some have floors; others do not. Some have curtains that can be dropped against the rain. Shop around, considering cost, weight, and design features that are important to your boat-camping lifestyle.

7
Getting in Gear

Clothing

Here are some nuggets concerning clothing for boat camping:

• Don't buy shorts or trousers with cuffs. They pick up sand, bugs, and debris that are brought back into the boat or tent.

• Women should avoid one-piece swimsuits, jumpsuits, underwear, or any other garment that requires major disrobing before going to the head. Toilets in boats and campgrounds are awkward enough to use without this added complication.

• Layer, layer, layer. No matter how hot and steamy it is at high noon, nights on the water can be chilly. During fly-in boating trips in Scotland and Holland we had to pack very lightly and yet be prepared for low temperatures and a great deal of rain. We found that a shirt or a blouse, topped by a wool cardigan, topped by a nylon windbreaker, kept us warm on the rawest mornings and yet could be reduced to shirtsleeve cool during the day. We tucked a lightweight rain poncho into a pocket.

It's more difficult to add layering under slacks, yet wool can get too hot during the day and jeans aren't warm enough on damp nights. Insulated underwear helps, but to remove it during the day can be awkward. One solution is to don leg warmers under slacks, then slip them out as the day gets warmer. Leg warmers can also be used on arms or tucked around a neckline on a raw day. It's best to buy slightly oversized slacks for ease of movement, ease of dressing, and room for adding insulated underwear.

• Few features are more important for warmth than a sewn-in hood with a drawstring around the face. A hooded sweatshirt topped by a hooded windbreaker provides double protection.

• New synthetic fabrics aren't at all like those of a decade ago. Because they keep you cooler or warmer and because they dry faster, they're often a better choice than natural fabrics. Shop in a store or a catalog that caters to serious campers, climbers, and yachtsmen to find the newest fabrics for outdoor wear.

Weatherproof Your Pack

As much as we'd like to have them, few of us can afford enough commercial dry sacks to hold every piece of boat-camping gear. An inexpensive, three-layer system will keep most gear clean and dry throughout your expedition. Carry extra plastic bags—you can never have too many for keeping gear waterproof, sorted, separated, and findable and for replacing bags that get torn or holed.

Place gear in cloth bags, which can easily be sewn at home, then in a plastic bag. Exhaust the air, using a soda straw if necessary to suck out the last few puffs of air. If the bag doesn't have a zipper top, seal it tightly with a rubber band. Then place it in a third, stronger bag, which will protect the tender plastic bag.

• Wool is warm even when it is wet. It's a good choice for cold-weather boat camping. Wool socks are cool in hot weather and warm in cold weather.

• A wool watch cap is a snug, warm, nearly waterproof choice for the coldest climates; in sunnier areas, buy a canvas hat with a brim and a chin tie. When it's clean and new, treat it with a good waterproofer, and retreat it after you wash it.

• When you are day boating out of a base camp, have a change of clothing on board for each family member if possible. Unexpected dunkings *do* happen!

• Have at least one extra pair of shoes for everyone aboard, so a dry pair is always available. Shower clogs are a must to keep you from picking up athlete's foot in marina and campground showers.

Sleeping Bags and Bedding

Typical in small powerboats is a four-seat layout in which seats are back to back, two facing forward and two facing aft. Each two-seat unit spreads out to form a single bunk. For these and other convertibles that have no separate mattress for tucking in sheets and blankets, sleeping bags are the best choice. No matter how you twist and squirm, your bedding can't come loose.

Sleeping bags are available in hundreds of colors and styles and in many price ranges and sizes. Despite their drawbacks, they're the easiest bedding to unroll each night and to stow each morning.

The Coleman catalog alone shows 31 sleeping-bag models, and the Peak 1 catalog shows 13—not counting numerous color choices and models that come in two weights. To say that choices can be confusing is an understatement! Snapping up a sleeping bag on sale at a discount store may not be the best choice for serious, long-term boat camping.

Here are some factors for you to consider when you choose a sleeping bag:

Weight. For canoe, kayak, and other featherweight boat camping the weight of the bag is a factor. There is no point in buying a five-pound bag for boat camping in the tropics.

Size. If you're extra tall or extra wide, buy an oversized bag. Few camping experiences are more wretched than sleeping in a bag that is too short. Sizes range from children's bags that are usually about 27" by about 57", to average sizes that are 33"–39" wide and 75"–79" long, to 85" extra longs that fit a seven-foot-tall person. For boat camping in cold weather, some people like to use an extra-long bag with room at the foot to store the clothes they'll put on the next morning.

Compatibility. If you want to zip two bags together, make sure that they are the same size and that their zippers are compatible.

Construction. Cheaper bags may be quilted in chain stitching, which begins to loosen after a few washings. The loss of this stitching allows insulation to drift around, wadding here and there to create cold spots and hot spots. Look for lock stitching throughout and for double and triple stitching at stress points. Zippers should work easily, should be corrosion- and rust-proof, and should be installed with guards that prevent snags and air leakage.

Look for a rolled top hem into which insulation has been evenly sewn. This prevents the insulation from drifting away from a top seam. At the bottom, box corners mean more foot space and easier zipping at the corner. If you need a warm bag, look for double batting—that is, insulation batts in two layers, one quilted to the cover and one to the liner. In single batting, voids at the stitching allow cold air to seep through.

Sleeping Bags at a Glance

Here's a summary, thanks to the Coleman Company, Inc.:

Types

A **Mummy** is just what it sounds like—a claustrophobic but very warm and practical bag for backpackers. A **Modified Mummy** is somewhat roomier. Some warmth is sacrificed in favor of more space. A **Barrel** is narrow at the foot and much wider in the chest and hip areas. The top often has a drawstring. Most popular is the **Rectangle**, which has a full zipper down the sides and around the bottom. Matching bags can be zipped together to make a double bag.

Fill

Goose down is warm, light, natural, long lasting—and expensive. It's comfortable in a wide range of temperatures but loses its warmth when it's wet. Synthetic fillers cost less, hold their warmth when they are wet, and are available in qualities that are much like real goose down. Synthetic fillers have a narrower temperature range, so sleeping bags should be chosen according to a comfort chart. Sleeping bags with both natural and synthetic fillers should not be stored in a compacted state. At home, hang them by the foot or store them loosely in spacious bags.

Cleaning

Wash sleeping bags no more than once a year unless it's absolutely necessary. Sleeping bags should not be dry-cleaned. Wash down bags by hand and with special soap. Most synthetic bags can be machine washed, but follow the manufacturer's directions. Always support a wet bag. Picking it up by one section or twisting it can tear its internal baffles. Both types can be put in a dryer on low heat. Put several clean tennis balls in the dryer with a down bag, as they'll keep the filling from clumping.

Fabric. Shiny taffeta and satin outer fabrics slip around too easily if you'll be sleeping on boat seats or cushions that are upholstered in plastic. Cotton duck gets a somewhat better grip.

Liner. Cotton flannel feels warmer to the skin, but it creates a little more "drag" on your body or garments than nylon taffeta if you toss and turn. A removable liner is a definite plus, because it can

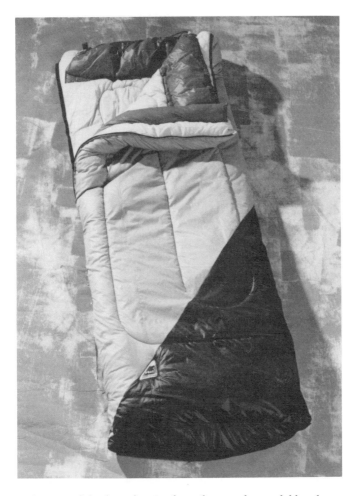

In this top-of-the-line sleeping bag, the popular model has been combined with high-tech features used in mummy bags. *Peak 1*

be laundered without washing the entire bag. The manufacturer may offer one as an optional extra. If it's well designed in a good percale fabric, it's a wise purchase because it will fit exactly and may have fasteners to keep it anchored. We've also made our own liners out of sheeting material. It's a simple matter to sew a rectangular sack, and we found it useful to incorporate a pillow pocket.

Washability. Look for a washable, preshrunk sleeping bag that does not require a special washing machine. On long trips you'll be using coin laundries. Flannel-lined cotton bags usually take longer to dry than do those made of a synthetic fabric.

Temperature rating. Sleeping bags are usually rated for mild (to the low 40s), cool (55° to the low 30s), cold (45° to the teens), or very cold (15° to −10° or so) temperatures.

Insulation. The cheapest bags use a solid-core polyester fiber. The more hollows in the fiber, the lighter and loftier the insulation and the more air is trapped for insulation. Dacron Hollofil 808 is a single-hole fiber, Hollofil II is a four-hole fiber, and Quallofil is a high-loft, seven-hole fiber. Thermaloft is a quick-drying, heat-trapping, low-bulk insulator often found in cold-weather bags.

Stowability. Cheaper sleeping bags come in a flimsy stuff sack that won't withstand constant repacking. Look for good compression straps, a sturdy stuff bag, or both.

Other Choices

Not all boat campers, of course, will choose traditional sleeping bags. Despite all of their good points, they are confining. You can't always zip into or out of them. In hot climates you broil because you can't peel away layers of blankets until you're down to one sheet. And they can make basic romantic endeavors more complicated. Other choices exist.

As shoestring campers we made our own bedding for many trips, using an old Girl Scout technique for folding sheets and army blankets together. Here's how you do it: Spread a blanket out flat on the floor. Place another blanket flat on top of it, but only overlap it by half. Place a third blanket atop the first and a fourth blanket or a sheet atop the second. You now have a double-thick bottom layer at the center, with half the remaining blankets on one side and half on the other. Now fold the blankets back across the center, alternating layers. Turn up the bottom and fasten it with big safety pins. For extra security you can also put a big pin on each side, about halfway from the bottom. You need to be able to fold back the top layers enough to squirm into the bag. You now have a single bedroll that is as warm underneath as it is on top and that won't come loose if you're an active sleeper.

In other boats we have wrapped sheets around the boat cushions and tied them in knots so they wouldn't pull loose. You can also do a great deal with sheet hold-downs, which are sold in sets of four in housewares departments. Each one is a piece of elastic with a gripper fastener (picture a garter belt) at each end. Giant safety pins can be useful too.

If you want to buy a bed system, Travasak is one of the best known. It's traditional bedding just like what you use at home—percale sheets, puffy comforters, and matching pillowcases, all available in pretty colors and in single, double, and larger sizes. Everything attaches together as one unit. The sheets are attached with Velcro, so it's easy to remove them for laundering. One nice feature is that the two sides are different weights. Put the light side on top for hot-weather sleeping, the heavy side up for cold-weather camping. Travasak is easy to roll up each morning and to flip across the bunk or tent floor each night. Found in catalogs including *Camping World,* it's a good choice for use on board or in a tent.

If you sleep on board and want bedding to fit an odd-sized bunk, Nautical Image (513–421–6951) specializes in top-quality custom work. Only the finest percales are used, to make bed systems that go on easily and fit perfectly. Features include fitted bottom sheets that cling to the mattress even though you can't get to all sides to tuck them in and fitted top sheets that slip over the bottom of the mattress and won't pull loose during the night. Also available from Nautical Image, if you're really into decor, are custom bedspreads and pillow shams and monogrammed towels.

Pillows

In a pinch, especially in flyweight boat camping, we simply seal up some air in a zip-top plastic bag and wrap it in a T-shirt. Inflatable pillows, which are available in camping-supply stores, save space and weight and can be wiped dry if they get wet. They're small enough to be inflated by mouth each night.

Mattresses

The most comfortable air mattresses are multicell types with a fabric-like coating, but it's cumbersome to carry a compressor or foot pump. It takes time to inflate them every night and even more time to wrestle them back into their stuff sacks in the morning.

We've spent wonderfully comfortable nights on nature's mattresses: a sandy beach or a nest of pine needles. In parts of Florida Spanish moss is also abundant enough to gather. Natural cushions can be buggy or highly allergenic, however, so they aren't for everyone.

===

Types of Foam

Closed-cell foam is good for support and for holding its shape. It does not absorb water.

Open-cell foam is soft and provides the most cushioning in pillows and pads.

In **laminates** a layer of soft, open-cell foam on the side that will touch the body is combined with an outside layer of firmer, closed-cell foam.

Premium foams are denser, firmer open-cell foams.

Reticulated foam is a very light material that lets air and perspiration pass through. It's a good choice for padding that is worn on the body, such as backpacks or knee protectors.

===

Fortunately, camping-supply outlets now offer a good choice of compact bedrolls in flat foam or "egg-crate" styles. The new closed-cell foam pads, such as Ensolite, are a good choice. They're comfortable and compact, and they require no inflation. Best of all, they can't absorb water the way open-cell foam can. If one gets wet, you simply sponge it off.

Linens

It pays to invest in 100 percent cotton or 100 percent linen dish towels because they'll dry dishes more thoroughly than will synthetics or blends, will launder better, and can be bleached when they become stained. We always take as many extras as possible because a clean dish towel always looks fresh when used as a table cover, a wrapper for hot bread, or a work-surface cover when assembling sandwiches.

Although it sounds silly to suggest that you starch tea towels to take on a camping trip, they really do stay clean longer if they are starched and ironed first. Seal up a stack of freshly ironed, spray-starched towels in a zip-top bag and see if you don't agree that it's worth the extra work.

Hand towels and bath towels should also be cotton. We prefer to carry a few medium-weight terry towels per person rather than extra-thick towels, which take forever to dry, or bath sheets, which are too big and clumsy to use in a small, wet shower cubicle with a dirty floor.

Don't forget to take pot holders and oven mitts, preferably the type with a scorchproof finish. We also take the biggest vinyl tablecloth we can find room for. It provides a clean work and eating surface on the ground or on campsite tables, which are usually rough and unappealing. Also, it is a big, waterproof cover we can use to cover the whole galley setup if we're caught in a sudden rainstorm. A tarp would do the same thing, of course, but a tablecloth in a pretty pattern looks cleaner and brighter in food-preparation areas.

A vinyl tablecloth can be wiped clean during the trip and put into a washing machine for a thorough cleaning. Wash it in the gentle cycle with a few terry towels to provide the scrubbing, and remove it before the spin cycle. Better-quality flannel-backed tablecloths are best because they stand up to hard wear yet remain supple. Cheaper vinyl table covers fall apart after a few uses. Oilcloth becomes brittle.

Lights

Redundancy is always a virtue, and lighting is one area of boat camping in which you can have many kinds of light at a small cost. In short, you want to use each energy source as efficiently as possible and to avoid carrying many different fuels and battery sizes.

If your boat has a 12-volt lighting system, make the most of that by installing lamps where they are most needed for cooking, checking the engine, reading in bed, and so on. If you install a plug at a central point in the boat and carry a 12-volt trouble light, you can have light anywhere it's needed.

In buying flashlights, choose as many different styles as you want (signaling, spotlight, floating, waterproof, red/green), but try to stay with the same batteries (D-cells, 6-volt) so you're not carrying an entire supermarket of sizes and types. Forget rechargeables unless you have a means of recharging them regularly. Rechargeable batteries need faithful attention and are not suitable for every boat-camping situation.

We also like each crewmember to have a small personal flashlight for reading in bed or finding a midnight snack. Again, many choices are available in AA and AAA models. Stick to one or the other,

New technology makes for better lighting from traditional gasoline lanterns. Lanterns also come in many new types and sizes. *Coleman*

preferably a battery size you're carrying for other battery-operated aids.

It pays to buy the latest and best lighting equipment rather than garage-sale stuff. With new, computer-designed reflectors, state-of-the-art krypton or halogen bulbs or fluorescent tubes, dramatically improved mantles, rustproof coatings, and tough carrying cases, new lanterns and flashlights burn more brightly, use less energy, and serve longer than did the models we used only a decade ago.

More than just a romantic whimsy, votive candles are a practical addition to your galley pack. Two or three of these lights provide enough brightness for dinner on a dark night, lighting up corners a campfire doesn't reach. They burn for hours, even in high winds, and refills can be carried in very little space. Candles also come in handy for lighting a campfire on a damp day. One match lights the candle, which keeps burning until the tinder finally catches.

In addition, we keep a few disposable chemical light sticks on hand. They stay dormant until they are activated and then burn until they expire, so they're only for emergency use.

It's hard to beat the classic camping lantern for dependability and fuel efficiency. Get lantern(s) that use a fuel you are carrying aboard for other purposes (Coleman fuel, propane, kerosene, D-cells, 6-volt lantern batteries, etc.). The new fluorescent lanterns and flashlights are available in battery models and in a rechargeable unit that can be charged in household or 12-volt outlets.

Knives

Chuck Buck is the fourth generation of a family whose products have long been on the cutting edge, so to speak, of knife technology for hunters, campers, and fishermen. We asked Buck what to look for in a knife that would do yeoman duty in boat camping. "We don't always have room to carry whole sets of knives," we explained. "We need one or two that will do everything from filleting fish to trimming strawberries."

"Many people prefer folding knives that lock open for safety," Buck responded. "Then the blade can be closed into the handle and carried in a compact package on the belt. We also have some customers who prefer the strength of a fixed blade. They usually ask for a blade about four to five inches long that can be used for fixing dinner, slicing meat, filleting fish, cutting vegetables, and, in some cases, skinning a rabbit or deer."

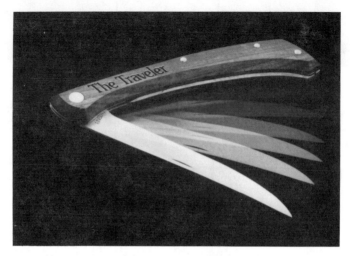

When you choose knives for boat camping, look for multi-purpose use and stowability. *Chicago Cutlery*

Buck's most popular all-purpose outdoor knife, called the Folding Hunter, is highly versatile. In addition, Buck recommends a smaller knife with a four- or five-inch blade for camp work, plus a light hatchet for cutting kindling. Buck makes a lightweight thermoplastic-handled Bucklite folding lockback knife with three- or four-inch blades for hikers, canoers, and others who pack with weight in mind.

Buck also makes a line of Tiny Titanium kitchen knives with serrated blades and the Selector series, in which three handles and nine blades fit in one rugged Cordura sheath. We also like the SwissBucks, which are available in 13 models. Made in Switzerland to Buck standards, they are multifunctional knives that can cut, file, saw, scissor, open cans, and so on.

The company also makes sharpeners. Buck offers these tips for sharpening a knife: (1) establish the correct angle on the stone and maintain it; (2) use an even, circular stroke and light pressure; and then (3) turn the blade over and repeat the process. Rotate the blade on the stone in a clockwise direction to avoid burring. Repeat this paired action until you have the edge you want. "Remember," he adds, "a dull knife is often more dangerous than a sharp edge." With

Boat-camping knives can be found in hardware and sporting-goods stores as well as in kitchen-supply departments. *Brunton/Lakota*

a proper edge, a knife cuts easily where you want it to, without awkward or forced motions.

Some other dos and don'ts about the all-important knives you use in boat camping:

- Wear your knife on a belt, well back on your thigh where it won't interfere with sitting or kneeling.

- Keep your knife in its proper sheath to protect both the knife point and your own skin. Keep the sheath snapped shut so you don't lose the knife.

- Don't put an unprotected knife into a storage box or drawer. Jostling and vibrations under way allow the knife to damage other items in the drawer, nicking and dulling the knife in the process.

- Clean and dry your knife after every use.

- Keep your knife sharp, cleaned, and oiled.

- Don't throw a fine knife—that's done only in movies.

• Don't use your knife for prying, screwdriving, or hammering.

For a booklet on *Knife Know-How* write to Buck Knives, Inc., 1900 Weld Boulevard, El Cajon, California 92020.

Binoculars

No matter how small the boat or light the pack, binoculars are a boating basic, not just for piloting the boat but for a full harvest of the sights nature provides along the way.

When you choose binoculars for boat camping, it's important to know why ordinary binoculars won't do. For one thing, boats move. For another, you need the best light-gathering qualities possible because there may be times when much depends on your ability to pick your way into port at night. Your choice must be a compromise among many features.

With thanks to Bushnell, the sports-optics division of Bausch & Lomb, here are some tips on choosing a pair of binoculars.

Exit pupil. The column of light that comes through the binoculars to your eye is determined by the power of the binoculars and the size of the front lens. If your glasses are 7×35, that means the exit pupil is 5mm in diameter (35 divided by 7). The larger the exit pupil, the clearer the image in low light.

Magnification. When you buy 7×35 binoculars, the 7 refers to how many times the image is magnified. You'll get more magnification in 10× glasses, but when the image is magnified motion is magnified too. So 7×35s are a good compromise for boating: they provide good magnification but can be used in an unsteady boat.

Objective lens. In 7×35 binoculars the 35 means that the front, or objective, lens is 35mm across. The larger these lenses, the sharper and brighter the view. So, in saving space by buying compact binoculars, you're also shrinking the size of the view available.

Prism systems. Two types of prism are used, porro and roof. Porro prisms generally give better depth perception.

Coated optics. Special coatings on all lens surfaces improve light transmission to give a brighter view with higher contrast. As a buyer, know whether all of the lenses in the binoculars are coated, or just some, and with what. Magnesium fluoride, plus coats of zirconium dioxide and aluminum oxide, may be used. Those with ultraviolet coating use cerium dioxide. Corners have probably been cut on coatings in cheap glasses.

Peak 1's Checklist

These are the items suggested by Peak 1 for backpacking and canoe camping. Starred items are essential for wilderness excursions.

Air mattress or pad
—Batteries
Camera, film
Camp shoes
Can opener
*Compass
Cooking utensils (2-quart pot, frying pan, cup)
Crampons
Dishpan, scrubbers
Eating utensils
*Emergency blanket
*Extra clothing
*Extra food
First-aid kit
*Flares, mirror, other signals
Flashlight
Fuel, funnel
Gloves
Ground cloth
Hammer (for tent stakes)
Hand ax (may replace hammer for tent stakes)
Hat
Hiking boots, hiking shorts
Insect repellent

Lantern, mantles
Lighter (disposable butane)
*Knife
*Maps
*Matches, waterproof case
Pad and pencil
Prescriptions
Rain suit
Rope or cord
Shovel (folding)
Sleeping bags
Snakebite kit
Soap (biodegradable)
Spatula, spoons
Stakes, stove
*Sunglasses
Suntan oil, lip balm
Tent, tent poles
*Toilet paper
Toiletries
Towels (paper and cloth)
Trash bags
Underwear, socks
Water bottle, water, purifiers
*Whistle

Additional Checklist

If you have more space, the Coleman Company's checklist contains these additional items:

Coffeepot
Cooler
Folding chairs, camp stools
Folding stove stand

Ice or ice substitute
Radiant heater
Tablecloth
Tool kit

The better the coating, the more glareproof the binoculars—a plus when you're trying to pick out a dark shoreline against bright lights or find a marker when you're looking into the sun.

Field of view. The field is the width of the area you can see at 1,000 yards. The wider the angle of the binoculars, the wider the area you'll see when you're scanning for wildlife.

Other features to look for are:

Waterproofing. Some binoculars are rubber coated, which cushions them from jostling, makes for better splash resistance, and assures a better grip when your hands are wet, but not all water-resistant binoculars are truly waterproof.

Built-in compass. This is a plus for navigation and for taking bearings.

Eyeglasses. If you wear glasses, it's a plus to buy binoculars that can be used without removing them. Some models have retractable eye cups or another design feature that makes them easier to use with glasses. Try for yourself.

Focus. Some binoculars are permanent focus, which can be a plus; others have a center focus, which is quicker than having to adjust each side separately. However, when you have a diopter focus adjustment for each eye, you can adjust for vision variations between your right and left eyes.

8

Electrifying News

If you boat camp without electrical aids of any kind ashore or afloat, skip this chapter. It's our guess, however, that you have at least some watts working for you somewhere. Most of us have many electrical accessories, from the exotic (a laptop computer, a 12-volt hair dryer) to the commonplace (lights, a radio, etc.).

Part of the fun of boat camping is improvising, innovating, substituting, and doing without. There are times, though, when only electricity will do the job. Let's talk about power management of all electrical gear, from the smallest flashlight right up through the luxury of shore power.

Rechargeable Batteries

Rechargeable accessories got off to a rocky start, and some boaters and campers still haven't forgiven them. Forget the days when rechargeables didn't have replaceable batteries at all. They were followed by models that were somewhat better but were still short on life and long on quirks. Today, however, many of the tools, toys, entertainment electronics, and galley gear that travel with us really are, or can be, rechargeable.

For boat camping, rechargeable batteries have obvious advantages, but they also have drawbacks. Here are some considerations.

• There's no question that rechargeable batteries are better for the environment. They can be recharged as many as 1,000 times. The hitch is that they need regular charging. Unless you have room to carry a charger on board or are boat camping for only one or two

Running Times for Batteries

Gates Energy Products gives the following typical running times to expect from batteries—depending, of course, on individual use. Read your owner's manual: times may be different for your unit.

Boom box	4 hours
Camera	150 flashes
Cellular telephone	24 hours
Electric shaver	14 shaves
Laptop computer	3 hours
Pager	2 weeks
Pencil sharpener	200 pencils
Personal radio	16 hours
Portable TV	3 hours
Tape recorder	6 hours

nights at a time, you'll get longer, better service from disposable batteries.

• Newer chargers are far faster than early ones. Solar chargers are available, and so are 12-volt rechargers that work off the boat's electrical system. You may be able to manage rechargeables even if you don't plug into shore power.

• If you're taking new rechargeable batteries on a trip, be sure to charge them first. They're usually sold in an uncharged condition.

• If batteries are changed very infrequently, such as the smoke-detector battery you change once a year, you're probably better off with throwaways. In appliances that require more than one battery, never combine rechargeables with throwaways.

• When you buy accessories with rechargeable batteries, look into the cost of replacing the batteries. Eventually, new rechargeable batteries must be purchased, and some oddball batteries are almost impossible to find. Try to make sure that your appliance won't be an orphan when its batteries wear out.

• In winter camping, keep batteries warm: chemical action slows down in cold weather. At zero degrees you'll get only about 40 percent of normal running time.

Marine Batteries

Even small boats these days commonly have two electrical systems on board, one to start the engine and another for the "house" (lights, radio, pumps, trolling motor). Because marine batteries are a major investment, it pays to get the right batteries to begin with and to manage them well for long life and untiring service. Here's how.

Buy the right size and capacity of battery. If your boat's original manufacturer skimped by supplying the smallest possible battery and battery box, it won't do the job after you've added a stereo, a 12-volt TV set, a horn, searchlights, and radios.

Add larger batteries if necessary. Physical size is not the only indicator. You're looking for the most amp hours for the dollar. Read the labels and the guarantees. If you've been using a start battery for deep-cycle service, the guarantee may not be honored.

Buy the right type of battery. There are two basic types of marine batteries. One is designed to give a high-powered, brief burst of power to crank an engine. A deep-cycle battery, by contrast, is engineered to deliver steady power over the long haul. Because different technology is required for each type of power, you need two separate batteries and electrical systems, one for the engine and one

---

Automatic Battery Switch

One way to keep both battery systems charged while making sure you can't discharge the start battery by using too many lights or radios is to use an automatic battery switch (ABS). One manufacturer is Wells Marine Technology, 2383 SE Dixie Highway, Stuart, Florida 34996. Models for two or more batteries are priced from about $130.

Under way, both batteries are charged. When the engine is shut down, Wells's patented sensor automatically isolates the start battery from the "house" battery. No matter how you abuse the "house" system, the start battery remains fully charged. If, for some reason, the cranking battery runs down from hard starting, the "house" battery can be manually switched into service. It's spring loaded, so it can't be left on accidentally. According to Jack Wells, the ABS can be installed by the average boatowner, without special tools, in less than an hour.

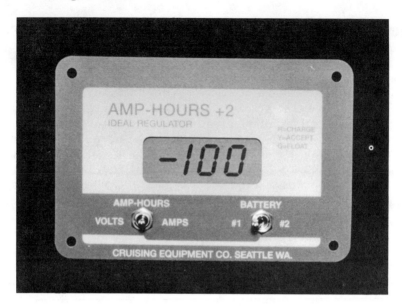

Batteries have to be managed just like a checking account: You can't take out more than you put in. Devices like this one help you manage your account. Called the Amp-Hours +2, it gives a digital readout of energy level, telling you when to recharge, how much charge is left, and when batteries are approaching the end of their useful life. It can be hooked to two batteries or to a battery plus an independent power source, such as a wind generator or a solar generator. *Cruising Equipment Co.*

for the "house" and/or trolling motor. One combination battery, the Stowaway, is designed to provide crank power for outboards and medium-sized inboards as well as deep-cycle service.

Install batteries correctly. Current is lost with distance, so it's best to install batteries as close as practical to the places where electricity will be used and where replacement energy will be generated. The batteries should be away from engine-room heat, in a protected spot that won't be damaged if acid leaks. You also want to keep batteries easily accessible for service, low to the boat's center of gravity, and where they can be well secured. Batteries are heavy.

Add water correctly. Most of us have maintenance-free batteries in our cars, so we tend to forget about them. But there are still many good batteries on the market that require regular checking and addition of water. The water in deep-cycle batteries, which take a hotter charge, is more likely to evaporate.

You may not realize, however, that it's as bad to add too much water as too little. Modern batteries have a reservoir with a visible filler scale at the bottom of the filler tube. Fill them too much, and they'll spill over when they warm up. Use clean, preferably distilled, water, because minerals and other contaminants settle on plates and weaken performance.

Keep batteries clean. As soon as you've filled a battery, clean up any spilled water. If you've filled and dried the battery correctly, that's all the cleaning you'll ever have to do. If you see green corrosion around battery posts, clean the lead parts with a wire brush. Don't use a wire brush on plastic cases, though—they should be cleaned with something softer, such as a moisture-dispersant spray (CRC 6–66, WD–40, LPS), and then wiped clean. Baking soda can be used to neutralize any spilled acid.

Stow batteries correctly. All lead/acid batteries self-discharge to some degree, and the process is speeded up by heat. The worst thing you can do to a battery at the end of the season is to store it in your basement next to the furnace or to put it away in a discharged condition. Charge it, then store it in a cool place (but not a concrete surface) where it won't freeze.

Charge batteries properly. Batteries should be charged as soon as possible after discharge. Keep a running score, as if your battery "account" were a checkbook. Take out more than you put in, and you'll be hit with a big overdraft penalty. You may also want to add a separate alternator to charge your "house" battery. It's best to have a manual control that allows you to bring start batteries back to full charge at a fairly heavy rate. Just be careful not to overheat them.

Deep-cycle batteries should be charged at a slow rate, says GNB Pro Marine, makers of Stowaway, Action Pack, and Super Crank batteries. Use a hydrometer to determine the state of charge.

Check the battery box. Batteries should be covered to prevent anything from falling onto them, but not so well sealed that corrosive gases stay inside, eating the battery. Batteries give off large amounts of hydrogen, so some provision should be made for venting them.

Battery boxes should also be kept clean. While you're at it, make sure the box is well secured, to prevent damage from vibration. Check the terminals to make sure they're not hitting anything that could short-circuit in bouncy seas.

Check the connections to make sure they're tight. And any time you're working near battery terminals, make sure they can't short to each other or to ground. A steel wrench between two terminals could turn red hot and burn you. So could a ring or a watch.

Simply put, the key to optimum battery life is to follow basic maintenance procedures, which vary according to the type of battery you have and the uses you make of it. There's still no substitute for reading owners' manuals and following them to the letter.

Solely Solar

Until some breakthrough is made, photovoltaic power will remain an expensive luxury. Still, the sun is a renewable resource that can be used indirectly to generate electricity or directly in solar cooking and to heat up a Sun Shower.

A complete guide to buying or building a solar cooker and cooking with it is *Cooking with the Sun* by Beth and Dan Halacy, which you can order from Morning Sun Press, Box 413, Lafayette, California 94549. The drawback, especially in hot weather, is that you must do all of your cooking during the worst heat of the day. The authors have achieved fantastic results, however, and their methods are fun to try, especially as a teaching tool for children.

Solar showers are available through camping- and boating-supply catalogs. The most compact, inexpensive, and practical are black bags with a shower attachment. You hang the bag in the sun until it's the desired temperature, then shower.

A fancier solar shower that hooks to a garden hose is available from Anello Brothers, Inc., 340 Route 23, Pompton Plains, New Jersey 07444. It's more practical for permanent installation in your privately owned campsite than for nightly off-loading and assembly. Other solar models are always popping up too, so keep browsing through the camping catalogs.

Indirect use of the sun through photovoltaic energy has some very practical uses in boat camping. Solar-rechargeable lanterns and tools are sold through such specialty catalogs as Real Goods, which also carries solar panels, solar vents, solar trickle chargers, and all other solar needs.

House Current

With today's technology offering so many small, efficient appliances, it's tempting to consider having refrigeration, a television, a blender or a food processor, and a few power tools in

More solar electric accessories are becoming available all the time. This solar-operated fan can be installed anywhere on the boat to improve ventilation. *Nicro Marine*

your boat-camping life. Household current costs more than many of us are willing to pay, however. We have three choices. One is to plug into shore power each night at a marina or a campsite. The second is to put up with the weight, fumes, space, maintenance, and incredible noise that go with a generator. The third is to use an inverter to silently turn battery power into 110-volt juice.

We'll mention a fourth choice only because it's available. Engine-driven alternators that provide 110-volt power are sometimes used in larger boats, but they aren't practical for most boat-camping applications. Their down side is that the electricity is available only when the engine is running.

Here are some thoughts about bringing 110-volt power into your boat-camping life.

• The cheapest, quietest, and simplest way to have electricity aboard is simply to plug into shore power. We've found that the most popular appliances in campgrounds and marinas are TV sets, electric blankets, and one or two electrical appliances:

Built-in Refrigeration

In Chapter 13 we discuss ice chests and portable 12-volt refrigerators. If you must have refrigeration on board, the best and most efficient system is a holding (eutectic) plate and an engine-driven compressor that is installed in a custom-carpentered box with very good insulation. Most users find that they need to run the engine for only about two hours a day with these systems. Another advantage is that the refrigerator can be made in any size or shape, to make the fullest use of available space. It's best to design a chest-type unit, with a top opening, to avoid losing cold air every time it's opened.

A second choice is a ready-made, RV-type refrigerator that runs on either household or 12-volt power. Such refrigerators have little or no holding power, so they must have a constant energy source. Because they come in standard sizes, they don't make the best use of available space. The disadvantage to any built-in is that you can't take it ashore to the campsite.

favorites include a coffee maker, a toaster oven, and/or an electric skillet. So if you want to use these luxuries, you may as well invest in a suitable heavy-duty, waterproof power cord.

• If you wire the boat to accept shore power, you can use 110-volt lights, an electric heater, galley appliances, computers, a battery charger, a charger for your rechargeable batteries, and so on.

• If you're docking *only* to plug into electricity, however, you're getting power at a very high price. Consider the shore-power option only if you like to dock nightly anyway for dinner ashore, for walking the dog, for letting the children run, or for some other reason.

• Inverters that change 12-volt battery power to 110-volt AC power are an inefficient use of your boat's battery reserves, but they do make sense for some boat campers. And new models give you much more energy efficiency, in a smaller unit, than did those of a few years ago.

Say you need power only occasionally to run an electric razor, a blender for a nightly daiquiri, or an electric tool for repairs. An inverter in the 120- to 200-watt range is an inexpensive, quiet way to convert battery reserves to household power.

Power Requirements of Some Popular Appliances and Tools

Heart Interface, makers of inverters that convert 12-volt battery power to 110-volt household juice, compiled this table to show what appliances and tools can be run on their 600-, 1,000-, and 1,800-watt inverters:

Appliance or Tool	Watts	Start-Up Watts	Minimum Inverter Needed
13" television	80	NA	600 watt
19" television	100	NA	600 watt
VCR deck	50	NA	600 watt
Stereo	50	NA	600 watt
Curling iron	50	NA	600 watt
Lamp	100	NA	600 watt
Blender	300	NA	600 watt
3/8" power drill	500	NA	600 watt
Small hand sander	500	NA	600 watt
Ice maker	200	1,000	1,000 watt
Small coffee maker	1,000	NA	1,000 watt
3 cu. ft. refrigerator	150	750	1,000 watt
Compact microwave	750	NA	1,000 watt
Full-sized microwave	1,500	NA	1,800 watt
Hand-held vacuum cleaner	1,100	NA	1,800 watt
Hair dryer	1,500	NA	1,800 watt

All the time you're under way, the battery is being recharged by the engine alternator. As we've said, it's a good idea on any boat, especially one that uses electricity for any living purposes, to have two complete electrical systems, one for the engine and a second for the "house." Otherwise you can use too many lights or watch TV for too long and not have enough battery power to start the engine again.

If your boat-camping style demands a generator, despite all the drawbacks of noise and fumes, the first step is to make a thorough inventory of your need for household power. You'll waste fuel if you run a generator only to watch TV, and it's bothersome to have to light the generator every time you want a cup of coffee.

Don't buy anything in a 110-volt model if it can be found in propane, battery, 12-volt, solar, mechanical, or other form. With persistent shopping in camping- and sporting-goods stores and catalogs, you can find all kinds of non-110-volt appliances, from butane hair rollers to a windup electric shaver.

Two types of generators are common in boating: water-cooled marine units and portable generators. The quietest, safest installation is a water-cooled marine generator in a well-insulated engine room, but few boats in our size range have that kind of space. In any case, buy a generator that uses the same fuel as the engine. There's no point in introducing a gasoline generator and gasoline fuel tanks if you have a diesel engine.

Carrying a portable generator is an inexpensive, easy, carefree alternative, especially if you off-load gear to sleep or eat ashore. Another advantage to a portable is that you can use it at home during power outages and around the yard to operate a 110-volt chain saw, a trimmer, a tiller, or other equipment.

A portable generator can be set up anywhere on deck or in camp where you have room and plenty of airflow. The more the generator is protected from the elements, especially salt spray, the better. And the more sound insulation you can provide between the generator and your own and your neighbors' living quarters, the better for everyone. In any event, running a generator won't win you any popularity contests, and it isn't permitted in some campgrounds.

Portables come in many sizes, from tiny generators just big enough to power a television set and a few lights to large units that can run almost an entire household. The smaller the unit, of course, the easier it is to carry and the cheaper it is to fuel.

It's tempting to scrimp on size, but don't be penny-wise and pound-foolish. You can damage the generator, as well as the appliance you're trying to run, by expecting it to put out more amps than it was designed for. To compute your needs, add up the amperage or wattage listings on all of the appliances you plan to use. (Every appliance or tool should bear a label with this information.) You need a list that is all watts or all amps. If the label lists only watts, divide by volts (110/115) to get amps. What you need to know is the total amperage or wattage your generator may be called on to deliver at once.

If you'll be using power tools, list the stalled amperage of each. Don't forget to add in the battery charger. You now have a summary of how many amps or watts you'll draw if you use everything at once.

You now have two options. One is to buy a generator big enough to handle it all. The other is to buy a smaller generator, then to ration generator use so that one appliance is turned off before another is turned on. Once you get the hang of it, it's not difficult, but everyone in the family has to be taught the system. It may not work for you. By buying a unit just a bit larger than your needs, you also leave room to add more electrical aids in the future.

9

Prepare to Repair

The more remote your boat-camping trips are, the more important it is for you to be self-sufficient. And if you've modified the boat, you'll need to be even more prepared for potential problems.

Here are suggestions for repair materials that can save the day when you are—pardon the pun—up the creek without a paddle.

Aluminum repair rod. You'll need a blowtorch to use it, so it isn't for everyone. However, a small propane torch is often near the top of our tool-kit list anyway. A durable weld can be made using only this rod, a torch, and a wire brush. Full instructions come with the rod, which is sold under such trade names as Lumiweld.

Clamps. You can keep almost anything together with small C-clamps until the glue dries or until you can make a better repair.

Dental floss. It's not just an essential in dental hygiene, it's one of the strongest threads you can use for emergency repairs to canvas, sleeping bags, upholstery, and other-heavy duty fabrics.

Duct tape. We hate to admit it, but this inexpensive, tough tape has held together more boat-camping trips than will ever be known. However, it's a poor substitute for proper tapes, which you should also carry: sail-repair tape, tent patches or tape, electrician's tape for repairing wires, and fiberglass-repair kits.

Goop. A clear goo that comes in a tube, not to be confused with a waterless hand cleaner that is also called Goop, this is a miraculous adhesive that stays supple after it cures. It bonds almost anything to almost anything else and can also be used to caulk leaks or plug small holes. We find it invaluable, especially for fixing leaky boots or reattaching flapping soles.

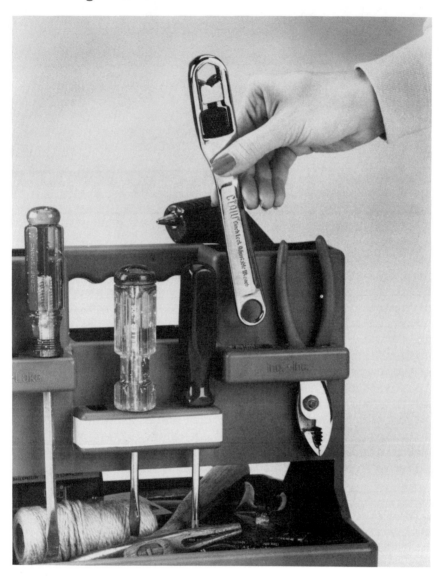

Choose versatile, multiple-use tools. One CLAW (Cinch Lock Adjustable Wrench) does the work of dozens of wrenches and sockets, standard and metric. *First Choice Tool Company*

Carry a good selection of the best-quality tapes for specific purposes. A proper rigging tape, for example, bonds to itself to form a solid piece of durable synthetic rubber. It can be used wet or dry, even underwater, and it can be removed only with a knife or scissors. The right masking tape, by contrast, is designed for temporary service and easy removal. *Mariner's Choice*

Ice pick. It's a must in the galley, but it also comes in handy in the repair kit as a hole punch.

Inflatable-boat repair kit. If yours is a good-quality inflatable boat, it probably came with a repair kit. If you don't have such a kit,

---

Tools for Everyone Whose Boat Has an Engine

Rock-bottom essentials
Screwdrivers of every size and type for which you have screws
Adjustable pliers
Needle-nose pliers / wire cutter
Wrenches to fit everything on your engine
Spark-plug socket wrench (buy a good one and try it at home—
    cheapies don't always work)
Spare V-belts in every size your boat uses, and any special
    wrenches needed to install them
Spare water-pump impeller
Moisture-dispersant spray (Lube One, WD–40, CRC–666)
Spare fuel filter
Spare shear pin if your engine uses one

Add these if possible
Scissors and gasket material or a tube of silicone gasket
Tube of sealant, preferably one that cures when it is wet
Single-edged razor blades (to chisel, cut, or scrape)
Voltmeter or a test light (if you have anything electrical aboard)

Nice but not always necessary
Equipment for one complete oil change
Pop-rivet set. It's quick and light for many types of fastening
Terminal pliers and extra wire terminals
File
Vise-grip pliers (they double as a clamp)
Hacksaw (for cutting wood, plastic, or metal)

---

buy one that contains materials and adhesives that are compatible with your boat.

Paddle. No matter how ungainly your sailboat or powerboat, you can probably propel, or at least maneuver, it with a paddle. We've seen Bahamian fishermen sculling their way home after their engines failed far out at sea, making good time even against the tide. We've also observed riverboatmen making their way to shore with the current, steering and paddling with an oar. An oar can also be used as an emergency rudder, fender, mast, ridgepole, or sunshade batten. If yours is a paddle-powered boat to begin with, carrying one or two extra paddles or oars is good insurance.

Sewing kit. Start with basic needles and threads, then add serious aids depending on your ability to deal with heavy-duty sewing repairs in sails, dodgers, tents, and the like. A thimble is a must for light-duty hand sewing; a sailor's palm is a necessity for pushing a needle through canvas.

Siphons. Have one for water and one for fuel, and keep them separate. Never use one for the other! Water could contaminate fuel. Worse, fuel could contaminate drinking water. We have used a siphon to fill our water jugs from springs and a fuel siphon in emergencies to transfer fuel between tanks or from a vehicle to the boat.

Small stuff. Every bosun's locker contains lengths of line in various sizes. They'll come in handy for extending, attaching, joining, holding, whipping.

Stainless-steel wire. Leader wire and other types of stainless-steel wire can be used to bind things together, to clean out carburetor passages (never put it in a jet), or to jury-rig a hose clamp.

Stove tools. Your stove may need a special tool kit to keep the burners clean.

III
The Cruise

10
Safety and Survival

Pat yourself on the back. As a boat camper you're more than a sailor and more than a camper—so you have the means of surviving both in the water and on land. Many a camper has come to grief for lack of a fire extinguisher or flashlight, which you, as a boater, have on board. Many a shipwrecked sailor has rued the day he or she was cast ashore without some landlubber essential, such as shoes, which you, as a camper, are sure to have. You have the best of both worlds.

According to MPI Outdoor Safety Products, 37 East Street, Winchester, Massachusetts 01890–1198, there are only five areas requiring basic survival skills: first aid, fire, body temperature, signals, and water and food. If you grasp their essentials, you'll be able to save lives. Come and explore them with us.

Self-Protection

The primary act of survival is taking care of yourself. Be prepared with a good medical kit. Keep it compact, lightweight, and readily accessible. Don't panic. Remember the S.T.O.P. rule: Sit, Think, Observe, Plan. Preplan by bringing rain gear, extra clothes, comfortable footwear, and survival and medical equipment. Review maps and guidebooks before you leave, and discuss your plans with people who know the territory.

Fatigue

Four hours of exposure to sun glare and heat, engine noise and vibration, motion through the water, and the pounding of the hull slow your reaction time to almost what it would be if you were legally drunk, says the Boat/U.S. Foundation. Add alcohol to the equation, and you have the recipe for the tragic crash in 1993 in which two Cleveland Indians players were killed when their high-speed bass boat hit a dock in the dark.

The more hours you spend in intense light and the less effective your sunglasses, the greater your loss of night vision. Bright sunshine, a bright boat, and sparkling water cause your eyes to protect themselves by dimming down. Just when you most need sharp eyesight—picking your way into a channel at dusk, searching for a marker at sundown, or towing the boat home on the highway—your vision may be half of what it was in the morning.

Protect yourself by wearing a wide-brimmed hat and large sunglasses with good ultraviolet-filtering lenses. Trendy little glasses that allow light to leak around the edges and at the nosepiece and have high-fashion color lenses are "fun" glasses, not sunglasses.

Fire

Fire can purify water, cook food, signal rescuers, provide warmth and light, help keep predators away, and warm the spirit—but it does require caution and precaution. Here are some tips:

- Practice alternative fire-starting techniques with a flint and steel, a bow drill, a magnifying glass, and whatever else you can think of.

- Have a supply of tinder on hand. An old Girl Scout trick is to save dryer lint and wrap it in a twist of waxed paper.

- Keep your supply of tinder and kindling dry under a space blanket.

- Learn the One Match, One Fire trick by lighting a candle, then using the candle to light the fire.

- Have two methods of starting a fire—such as dry matches plus a magnesium fire stick—with you at all times.

- Build fires where they can't cause a forest fire or be put out by melting snow or a rising tide.

- For warmth, protection against predators, or signaling, several small fires are better than one large one.

- To conserve fuel, make a "star" fire, with the ends of large logs in the center, and push the logs in only as needed.

- Use reflectors, such as aluminum foil or the shiny side of a space blanket, to increase heat and light.

- If possible, build the fire in a pit to make it more manageable.

What Smoke Detectors Can and Can't Do

Today's smoke detectors are so compact, energy efficient, and affordable that every boat with an enclosed cabin can have one. How can you make a smoke detector work for you?

First, to understand what it can and can't do, read the manufacturer's directions. The smoke detectors aboard your boat must be installed in the right spots to sense danger as early as possible, should have good batteries, and should be kept free of dust, usually by cleaning the sensing chamber once a year. Don't put yours where combustion particles normally occur—near a heater, where cigarettes are smoked, near an exhaust—or on any outside surface that is subject to extreme temperature changes.

Test the detector regularly, preferably each time you take the boat out. Some models are tested by passing a flashlight beam over a sensor; others have a push button. A good battery test doesn't mean that the smoke sensor is operating. Use the proper test mode.

Smoke detectors:

- Can't differentiate between good smoke and dangerous smoke. If you have too many false alarms from cooking odors or cigarette smoke, buy one of the silenceable models made for kitchen use. By pressing a button you can put such a detector into a pause mode, in which a beep sounds only once a minute. The mode lasts for about three minutes, then normal alarm function returns unless the silencer button is pressed again.

- Can't sense fires in other, separately enclosed parts of the boat. Put units where they'll be quickest to sense smoke from each cabin or other area.

- Can't work without power. Change batteries often. Most models have some type of low-battery warning signal.

- Can't alert the deaf, sound sleepers, or anyone who is drunk or drugged. Extra-loud models are available, but even these may not be heard through a closed door. Also available are models with a remote buzzer that can be rigged, say, in your tent to tell you there's a fire in your boat.

- Can't substitute for fire insurance. Warranties do not include replacement of property lost in a fire.

- Can't last forever. Smoke detectors are fairly complicated and should be replaced every 10 years, according to the manufacturers of First Alert detectors.

- Can't be interconnected unless they're made to be. Stand-alone units should not be modified or linked with any other devices. If you want a detector system that is interconnected by wiring or by radio signal, buy a unit that was designed for that purpose.

- Can't sense all fumes. You'll need other sensors to alert you to gasoline fumes, propane leaks, or carbon monoxide.

Carbon Monoxide

The kids in a family we know were napping below while their parents trolled the afternoon away. By the time the parents realized that the kids were unusually cherry cheeked, a tragedy was in the making. Unseen exhaust fumes had been trickling back into the cabin, poisoning the children with invisible, odorless, deadly carbon monoxide, or CO.

Even if you have an engineless sailboat, don't stop reading just yet. Anchored in a mountain lake where other boats are softly running generators, you too can be a victim. A couple once told us they had awakened on a still night on such a lake, and suddenly everyone started vomiting and complaining of headaches. Exhaust fumes from the generator on a neighboring boat had settled on the surface of the water and seeped into their boat.

Never use a heater, a lantern, a portable generator, or a stove in an unventilated tent or cabin. Charcoal cookers should be used only in the open. Even under a tarp that is open on all sides, CO fumes can cause illness in some people.

Janet had CO poisoning once, but it was a long time before she realized why she heard ringing in her ears and had splitting headaches. Other boaters tell us that they have been poisoned too but that at first they thought they were just seasick or had had too much sun. That's the worst part of CO poisoning—you may mistake the symptoms. Some victims take on a bright red or dusky color; others seem confused or cranky. Their pupils may be dilated.

Sad to say, CO attacks the youngest first. However, parents have time to act before they too are overcome, if they recognize the symptoms and act immediately. Anemic people succumb faster than do those with normal blood; smokers fall victim faster than do nonsmokers.

It is better to prevent CO poisoning than to treat it. The most common culprit is an exhaust leak, and the most common place to find a break in the exhaust line is at the joints. Seal any openings between the cabin and the engine room (usually places where plumbing pipes or electrical wires run through). Tighten the bolts that hold the exhaust manifolds to the engine, and examine the entire exhaust line for signs of cracks, drying, stress, or loose connections. Double-clamp exhaust hoses.

Even if your exhaust system is in perfect shape, fumes can be drawn into the cabin by the "station-wagon" effect. When you're speeding through the water a slight vacuum is created inside the boat, so exhaust is sucked below. The fumes don't reach people who are on deck, but someone who is sleeping below could be in danger. For children, dangers are doubled. When you're under way in a powerboat, make sure plenty of fresh air is channeled below from ahead, not astern.

Sophisticated new electronic CO detectors are now available, and they're a wise addition to any boat. Keep in mind that smoke detectors and gas sniffers can't sense CO. You must have a detector that is designed specifically for CO.

What if you suspect CO poisoning? If you feel nauseated, if you're dizzy, if you have a headache, or if your ears are ringing and you're in the presence of any device that could be producing CO, consider it the possible culprit. If you find someone unconscious in your boat or tent and there's no obvious injury, list CO among the suspects.

Immediately get plenty of air for yourself and the victim. Stop the engine or shut off whatever devices are producing fumes. Open hatches and tent flaps. If the victim is unconscious, broadcast a Mayday or otherwise get immediate help. Tell rescuers that you suspect CO poisoning: a victim can be helped sooner if oxygen can be supplied, and sooner still if a pressure oxygen chamber is available. While you wait for help to arrive, keep the victim warm and apply mouth-to-mouth resuscitation if necessary. CO poisoning is as rare in boat camping as it is in cars and at home, but keep it in mind nevertheless.

Fire Extinguishers

If your boat has an inboard engine, a permanently installed fuel tank, or a closed compartment carrying portable fuel tanks, U.S. Coast Guard regulations require you to have a B–1 hand-portable fire extinguisher aboard. Boats under 26 feet need one, and larger boats are required to have more, but no law says you can't have one or two even on a small sailboat with no engine.

In boat camping, with its cook stove and campfires, it's wise to have an extinguisher plus some other fire emergency aces up your sleeve. One of our favorites is a box of baking soda. It's no substitute for a proper extinguisher when you have a serious fire, of course, but when a cooking flare-up was getting out of hand, we scattered the soda over it and quashed the fire while saving the steaks. If we had set off the chemical extinguisher, it would have taken hours to clean up the resulting mess.

Comic Jay Leno tells a story about trying to bake potatoes for his birthday dinner. He had a grease fire in the oven, put it out with a fire extinguisher, and then was sick all night because he scraped the goo off the baked potatoes and ate them. Not a good way to spend a birthday! Baking soda, unlike chemical foams, can be washed off without leaving a dangerous residue.

A space blanket can also be used to smother a small fire.

Remember to position your fire-fighting equipment so you won't have to reach through the fire to get at it. Old-time campers always have a camp shovel, and perhaps a bucket of dirt, at hand to smother an overly ambitious fire.

It's commonly said that an alcohol fire can be extinguished with water. Technically, that's true, but throwing a bucket of water on a puddle of burning alcohol will probably scatter it into a dozen smaller puddles of burning alcohol.

Body Temperature

MPI puts it succinctly: anything that takes away from or adds to your body's ideal temperature of 98.6° can be considered an enemy.

In cold weather, wear layered clothing. If you don't have a hat, improvise one. Keep dry: wet clothes lose 90 percent of their insulation value. Avoid sweating. Use a space blanket. Watch for signs of hypothermia (shivering) and frostbite (white patches on the skin).

In hot weather, wear light colors to reflect sunlight away from your skin. Cotton fabrics are best. Always wear a hat. Make shade somehow—say, with space blankets.

Choose a shelter site that is safe from new hazards, such as trees that might fall or creek beds that are subject to flash floods. Don't waste time building a shelter if nature has provided one. Remember to insulate yourself from the ground as well as from cold air, rain, and wind. On treeless shores or islands, turn the boat over and dig a hole under it. In the forest, cut boughs and angle them out with their bases lashed to the trunk of a large tree.

Hypothermia

Still one of the most misunderstood hazards in boating and camping, hypothermia is more than just feeling cold. It is a chilling of your body's core (brain, spinal cord, heart, and lungs) to the point that your arms and legs become numb and useless. At the same time your brain numbs and you lose the ability to plot your own rescue even if an obvious solution is at hand. Hypothermia is sinister and deceptive, not at all what you might expect.

We once met a Tennessee boater who was so hypothermic when he made it back to shore after a series of problems that he had difficulty unlocking his car door and starting the engine. Relief was at hand, as soon as he could warm up the car and start the heater, but with numb hands and a befuddled brain the task was almost insurmountable.

Your survival time in water depends on two things: the temperature of the water and the speed with which your body loses heat. The water doesn't even have to be icy. Anything colder than a balmy 78° or so will eventually rob your body of heat.

If you're huddled in a fetal position, safely afloat in a Type I or Type II life jacket, you can last twice as long as you can if you try to swim. If you can huddle with other victims, or if you're wearing a float coat with insulation in the groin area (where heat loss is dangerously rapid because blood vessels are close to the surface), survival time will be longer.

Drownproofing, a popular technique often taught to nonswimmers, will deplete body heat fastest of all, because the head is constantly wet.

According to the Boat/U.S. Foundation, here is what to do if you find yourself in cold water:

Don't panic. Don't try to remove your clothes or shoes. Button up, zip up, and cover your head if possible. A little water trapped inside your clothing will provide some insulation. Stay as still as possible. The more you flail about, the more quickly you'll lose any air that is trapped in your boots and clothing and is thus helping to keep you buoyant. If possible, put on a personal flotation device (PFD). The more actively you swim or tread water, the faster your heat loss will be. Don't try to swim unless help is very close.

Devote all of your time to getting out of the water—onto a raft, a surfboard, or anything else that floats, even if it's a capsized boat or a boat filled with water. Remain as still as possible even if you're shivering and in pain.

If you pull someone from the water, assume that hypothermia is present to some degree. The first symptom is shivering, followed by loss of coordination, slurring of words, mental confusion, skin that is cold and blue, weak pulse, irregular heartbeat, and enlarged pupils. Find some way to warm the body with blankets or a hot-water bottle. Strip off wet clothes swiftly, with as little motion as possible, and put the victim, face up, on a blanket or other insulated surfaces. Work quickly.

Being careful not to burn the skin, apply gentle heat to the head, chest, neck, and groin. Don't heat arms and legs—that forces the cold blood back to the heart, lungs, and brain, lowering body core temperature even further. This additional "after-drop" can be fatal.

Don't rub the skin or give the victim a hot bath. Roughness may cause cardiac arrest. Don't try to give hot liquids to anyone who is unconscious, and never give alcohol to a hypothermia victim. Alcohol dilates the smallest blood vessels, sending a surge of blood to fingers and toes but robbing the body core of vital heat even further.

In extreme cases, wrap yourself in a blanket or sleeping bag with the victim, sharing your body heat. Whenever possible, of course, professional medical help is the rule.

Start CPR and don't give up; a person who has been in cold water and appears not to be breathing may revive. Miracles have happened, even to people who have been underwater for up to an hour.

The Sudden Disappearance Syndrome (SDS) is something else again. We've all heard of tragedies in which someone fell or jumped into the water and failed to surface. Sudden immersion, especially

Make the wearing of a PFD a privilege that identifies each child as a proud member of your crew. *National Marine Manufacturers Association*

in cold water, can lead to cardiac arrest or other problems. The only defense against SDS is to wear a PFD.

Life Jackets

According to the Boat/U.S. Foundation, the most important life jacket is the one you will *wear.* And that may not be the one the U.S.

Coast Guard requires you to have on board to pass inspections. Meet the letter of the law, but wear the buoyancy device that gives you the comfort you want.

Knowing how to swim won't protect you. As we said, if you fall overboard in cold water and try to swim, you'll hasten the deadly effects of hypothermia. You could be knocked unconscious as you go overboard too, or suffer cardiac arrest. Because four out of five people who die in boating accidents were not wearing PFDs, it makes good sense to wear one as much as possible.

Type I, or offshore, life jackets have a minimum buoyancy of 22 pounds for adults and 11 pounds for children. Because they can turn most people face up even if they're unconscious and can keep them afloat, they provide the greatest protection. But they're also the most bulky and uncomfortable. Most people will give them a thumbs-down for everyday wear.

Type II, or nearshore, buoyancy vests have a minimum buoyancy of 15.5 pounds and will turn most people face up in the water. They are less bulky than Type I but still offer considerable protection.

Because children's body weight is distributed differently, they are more likely to float face down in the water unless they're wearing the right PFDs. I once had to jump into a swimming pool, fully clothed, to fish out a four-year-old who was wearing a children's swim aid in the form of a big, buoyant bubble strapped to her back. It kept lifting her back out of the water and forcing her face into it. Panic set in, and it was downhill from there.

Type III vests are classified as flotation aids, but they should be worn only if rescue can be expected within a short time. They aren't designed to hold your head out of the water, so you'll have to expend energy to stay afloat. They're available in vest style or as jackets with sleeves.

Type IV devices are the throwables that must be carried, in addition to PFDs, on boats 16 feet and larger. The familiar buoyant pillow with straps is one type; the classic life ring is another. They help buy time, and they can be aimed more accurately if you're trying to throw flotation to someone in trouble in the water, but they're no help to people who are unconscious and little help to children and nonswimmers.

Type V hybrid devices have 7.5 pounds of built-in buoyancy and are inflated to 22 pounds when a carbon-dioxide cartridge is activated. They too require some cooperation from the victim, both to set off the charge and to keep the head above water. The jacket alone won't do it. Stylish and comfortable, hybrids are a popular choice among fishermen, white-water sailors, and those who want a built-in sailboard harness. To meet Coast Guard requirements, hybrids must be worn at all times.

Even though Types III, IV, and V are usually chosen for style as well as function, it's best to select bright colors such as orange or yellow rather than fashion colors. Until an MOB (man overboard) accident has happened to you, you don't realize how quickly a body can become invisible in the water. Add waves, sea-foam, low light, and a sun streak to the equation, and you can lose sight of the victim in seconds. By staying with high-visibility colors you add one more element of safety.

If you boat camp with a dog or cat, pet lifesavers are important too. Most pets swim instinctively, but heartbreaking accidents do happen. If you don't think your kind of boating calls for a PFD for your pet, consider putting it into a harness rather than a collar. If it falls overboard and you have to fish it out of the water, you can injure it by lifting it by the collar. A harness forms a safer lifter.

Floaters

In addition to the life jackets you wear, those you have stowed, and those you keep handy on deck (cushions, rings, horseshoes), keep in mind that many other items will float. The more things that remain afloat in a sinking, the more things you'll have to hang onto or climb up on and the more visible your plight will be to rescuers.

When you have seat cushions made for your boat, specify closed-cell foam instead of the cheaper open-cell foam. Not only does it float, it dries quickly after a rain because it doesn't absorb water. One brand is Airex, which is available by the square foot from Sailrite, 305 West Van Buren Street, Columbia City, Indiana 47625 (800–348–2769).

One of our friends, a single-hander aboard a tiny sailboat, was sleeping at sea under self-steering when his boat was sliced in two by a freighter. He woke up clinging to a large, closed-cell foam cockpit seat. It saved his life! Except for a few splinters, his boat and all of his possessions had vanished.

The more likely you are to capsize or to take a knockdown, the more important float packs become. Many white-water rafters have lost precious gear when a raft capsized. For the rest of the trip they had nothing but floaters plus any other lashed-down items that did not break loose. In many types of boating, getting soused is expected and planned for. In all others, it's always a possibility.

No waters in the world are more serene, safe, and shallow than the spring "runs" of Florida. In some spots only a few inches wider than a canoe, they tunnel through the forests under canopies of trees. The spring-fed streams flow at no more than three or four knots, and the water stays mirror flat even when the wind is screaming overhead.

It's one of the last places we'd worry about keeping gear in a float pack, but Murphy's Law struck again. Our friends, who were following us in another canoe, maneuvered around a very tight corner, crouched to conn the canoe under a big tree that had fallen across the stream, and suddenly found themselves face to face with a 10-foot-long alligator.

They lost it. They were fortunate that their gear was in a float pack, because their first priority was to get back on board and as far away from that gator as paddles and panic would take them. When the music stopped, they were able to retrieve their float pack and continue on their way.

When we're at sea, one of our MOB rules is to toss overboard almost anything that floats (cushions, ice chests). The higher the seas, the more help you'll need in finding the victim. A trail of floaters creates a path you can follow.

Signals

Having the ability to signal rescuers is your link to any available help, says MPI. Tricks you can use include:

- putting three fires in a triangle or in a straight line;

- on a clear day, making smoke with wet leaves or oily rags (at night you need bright fire, not smoke);

- setting off a red flare, but only if you know someone can see it (save the white flare for acknowledging);

- with an emergency light, sending six long flashes per minute, then pausing one minute, then repeating the pattern (under Inland Navigation Safety Rules a high-intensity light flashing at regular intervals from 50 to 70 times per minute is considered a marine distress signal, according to the Coast Guard); and

- if you don't have flares or a strobe, using light sticks or a flashlight, plus reflectors—in sunlight, use a reflecting mirror; a space blanket or aluminum foil also serve as a reflector.

When you're trying to attract searchers who are in the air, trace out a large V pointing to your position. Or make a large circle at least 10 feet in diameter. Tramp down snow or vegetation, or arrange clothes and gear in a V or a circle. Both are universally understood "help" signs.

Make noise, using a whistle or your boat's horn. Sound can carry for miles, especially in the quiet times at daybreak or dusk, in fog or mist, or in a heavily forested area. SOS, which is dot-dot-dot, dash-dash-dash, dot-dot-dot, is a universally understood signal for help. So are six long blasts over a one-minute period, one minute silent, then repeat. Don't shout without good reason. You'll just lose your voice.

Flares

You're required to have visual distress signals aboard. Boats participating in certain organized events, recreational boats less than 26 feet long, open sailboats of less than 26 feet with no engines, manually propelled boats, and boats on waters less than two miles wide are exempt. When in doubt, get a copy of the *Federal Requirements for Recreational Boats* from the U.S. Coast Guard, Department of Transportation, 2100 Second Street SW, Washington, DC 20593–0001.

Keep in mind that any pyrotechnic devices (hand-held flares,

"U.S. Coast Guard Approved" is a misunderstood phrase. The Coast Guard "approves" only those items it requires you to have aboard, and its "approval" means that the product meets or exceeds minimal requirements. In addition to these needs, you can have many useful, non-"approved" items that will make boating safer and more fun.

You may also find products advertised as "meeting Coast Guard requirements." Often this means that the product is as good as or better than it must be but that the manufacturer didn't go through all the red tape required to get approval. You have, of course, no assurance that such a product does meet requirements. U.S. Coast Guard–approved items, by contrast, have certification numbers on every unit.

meteors, parachute flares) or nonpyrotechnic items (flags, electric distress lights) must be U.S. Coast Guard–approved, current, in working order, and stowed where they're easily accessible. If these requirements aren't met, you could be cited.

If you have children aboard, be careful in choosing a safe yet accessible spot for storing such devices. An army-surplus ammunition box is good—and it can be fitted with a padlock.

Two warnings. First, in some states launchers are considered firearms. If you boat camp interstate, make sure you aren't violating gun laws. Second, never set off a visual distress signal or any other SOS device for fun.

If you want to practice by setting off flares or smoke signals that are past their expiration dates, do so with the official sanction of a yacht club or other group—that way the authorities can be notified. Club events of this type can benefit the entire family, because adults and older children can get the hands-on feel of handling flares safely and knowing exactly what it takes to ignite them.

Emergency strobe lights can be tested any time, down below or anywhere where they can't be seen and interpreted as a call for help. Specific rules govern testing an EPIRB. They're included in the operator's manual that comes with the unit.

Water and Food

Water deprivation won't be a problem for those who boat camp in freshwater, but we'll pass along MPI's recommendations for those who boat in seawater:

In a survival situation, you can last much longer without food than without water, so never wait until you're without water to collect and store it. You need between two and four quarts of water each day to replenish what you lose through respiration, urination, and sweating. Try to drink only in the cool of the evening. Never drink seawater or urine.

MPI suggests places to find water: streams, ice melt or snow melt, rainfall, in the ground, and in certain plants. Follow game trails, look for lush vegetation, or follow grain-eating birds. To reduce the risk of pollution—chemicals, giardia, parasites, bacteria, and viruses—strain the water through a handkerchief, then boil it for 10 minutes plus one minute for every 1,000 feet above sea level. Although this doesn't remove chemical pollutants, it kills organisms. Write to MPI for an explanation of how to make a drip still using a space blanket, a container, and a hole in the ground. Solar stills are also available through marine catalogs.

As for food, MPI suggests taking care of your shelter, water, and signaling needs first. "Always assume you may need some extra food and water when you plan your trip," MPI stresses. Have a survival kit, but don't use it except for *survival.*

For more information about the innovative survival aids made by MPI, write to the company (see page 93) or look for its products in outdoor and sporting-goods stores.

Thunder and Lightning

Afternoon thunderstorms are a way of life during the dog days. Hot, wet air rises from the earth's surface and collects angrily overhead. Even the most experienced sailor or camper has been surprised by squalls that seem to come from nowhere and aren't spotted until they're overhead. Frontal activity is easier to forecast, but it too can spawn unexpected squalls, tornadoes, and waterspouts.

It's important to get good forecasts before you launch, then stay in touch as much as possible by listening to weather radio, watching weather signs for yourself, and keeping an eye out for any storm signals and flags that are flown in your area.

The National Weather Service no longer uses storm flags and nighttime light signals, but many marinas and yacht clubs do. They're not only a salty and nostalgic touch that adds class to a marina, they're a courtesy that can benefit passing boaters who have no radio.

A triangular red pennant indicates a small-craft warning. Two red triangles indicate a gale warning. A storm warning is signaled by a square red flag with a black square in its center. Two such flags tell you a hurricane is due.

At night it may be difficult to pick out signal lights against background lights unless you know what to look for: three lights mounted vertically on a pole. A red light over the white is a small-craft warning. White over red is a gale warning. Red over red is a storm warning. Red-white-red is a hurricane warning.

Any thick, dark cloud is good reason to head for safe harbor. Once a storm hits, winds can suddenly switch and shriek, turning sails into pile drivers and churning the sea into a cauldron. No boat is immune, no waters are too small to escape the wrath of nature at its worst: downpours, tornadoes, waterspouts.

If you're too far offshore to get to shelter and must ride out the bad weather, all your best seamanship must come to the fore. At its simplest, the drill includes:

- Insist that everyone aboard don a PFD.

- Secure all loose gear, and close hatches. There won't be time once the storm hits. Winds don't increase gradually; they usually clobber you suddenly, and often from an unexpected direction.

- Get a fix on your location and the course to the nearest shelter. You may lose visibility completely. Before things close in, have an idea of where you are in relation to other boats and to marine hazards.

- Shorten or drop sail, start the engine if you have one, and head into the wind at idle speed. Try to keep some way on.

- In most boats, heading into the wind is the most stable position. If the propeller comes out of the water when you head directly into the waves, steer off a few degrees to one side or the other until you can keep the propeller biting.

A very good guide for powerboaters is *Fast Boats and Rough Seas,* by Dag Pike; canoers might read *Raging Rivers, Stormy Seas,* by Terry Storry, Marcus Bailie, and Nigel Foster. A good marine bookstore can recommend many books on heavy-weather sailing for your type of boat and boating.

To learn more about weather, read Ingrid Holford's *The Yachtsman's Weather Guide* and Alan Watts's *Instant Wind Forecasting.* Both are available from Sheridan House, Inc., 145 Palisade Street, Dobbs Ferry, New York 10522.

When lightning starts, it's especially terrifying because your boat is usually the tallest object around. To make things worse, it probably has a mast or radio antenna that reaches skyward and just begs to be struck.

Lightning kills some 500 people each year, many of whom are on small boats. In addition, millions of dollars in damage is done to boats. Once, while anchored in Biscayne Bay, we were so close to taking a strike that our hair stood on end and the air virtually crackled with electricity.

It's difficult to envision the immense power of lightning, which can focus a million volts on one small mast or antenna. At all costs, avoid it—no preventive guarantees 100 percent protection. Even if you don't take a direct hit, lightning can wreak havoc with your electrical system, any metals aboard, or your compass.

Because lightning explodes out of a cloud and seeks the likeliest path to ground, the essence of lightning protection is to help the bolt get to ground as quickly as possible, via a route that will do the least possible harm to you, your crew, and your boat.

If yours is a powerboat, its highest point is probably the VHF antenna, but don't count on that as a lightning rod because it's connected only by the flimsy antenna cable that goes to the radio. Buy an antenna that can be lowered during lightning conditions. Use the flag mast as a lightning-rod mount, adding a stainless-steel or brass ¼-inch rod that comes to a point, connected with No. 8 AWG copper cable to an underwater copper grounding plate, using the most direct route possible.

This grounding plate, which should be at least a square foot in size, can be the hull itself if it is metal, a propeller, a metal rudder or keel, or a radio-grounding plate (most VHF installations don't use them). If necessary for a straight route, add a grounding plate—if a bolt of lightning hits a sharp bend, it may go its own way.

If yours is a sailboat, standing rigging and sailtracks should be grounded according to American Boat and Yacht Council (ABYC) standards. On open daysailers, shrouds and backstays should be grounded. To protect the crew the ABYC recommends that any continuous metallic track on the mast and boom be connected at the lower or forward end of the grounding system.

The area that can be considered safest aboard your boat is a cone of protection that extends 60° from the vertical, from the highest point of whatever mast has the lightning rod. (On a powerboat, this is the flag mast). To be conservative, don't count on the full 60°, because not all storms hit from directly overhead.

Using elementary math, calculate what the cone of protection is aboard your boat. Then, if your boat is longer than the area protected by the cone, consider adding lightning rods at other spots, such as the bow flag mast or metal stern davits, to create overlapping cones of protection.

During a lightning storm, stay away from your radio and everything else you can avoid using, including spotlights or metal downriggers. Lower any antennas and anything else that is taller than your lightning rod. Even if there are lightning protectors in the radio-antenna lead, you'll have added protection if you disconnect the antenna from the radio. Some boaters recommend connecting it to a ground plug. (Don't ever try to transmit without an antenna in place, though—you could damage your radio.)

No precautions are surefire. On its way through your boat, lightning may decide to take a detour through a metal boathook on deck or even through a wet rib in a wooden boat.

Here are some precautions suggested by the ABYC:

- Find a safe harbor, where towers, buildings, bridges, or other boats are taller than you are.

- As much as is practical, stay inside a closed boat. By all means, be aware of the shape of the cone of protection and stay inside it.

- Try not to touch two metallic items, such as the gear lever and the spotlight, at the same time.

- Don't jump overboard.

- If your boat is struck by lightning, immediately check it for damage. If a through-hull fitting was blown out, you may be sinking fast. Don't rely on your compass until you've checked its bearings.

Camping High and Dry

In coastal camping, camp well above the highest high-tide line. Tides in the tropics are modest, but even in Florida and the Bahamas, where tidal ranges are only a foot or two, spring highs can catch you by surprise. In areas of more dramatic tides, such as Maine or Oregon, fast-moving tides can swirl around headlands and strand you in minutes.

In camping along rivers that carry commercial traffic, keep in mind that unexpected wakes from passing towboats can flood a campsite that is too close to the water. If the waterway is controlled by a dam, ask whether you should expect the water level to be raised or lowered during your camp-out.

In inland boat camping, avoid lowlands that are subject to flash floods. A pleasant creekside campsite that is sheltered by cliffs or big hills could become a raging torrent within hours, not just during heavy rains but also during snow melt.

Water levels can be changed in bays and basins by constant winds or changing barometric pressures that push the water off one shore and onto another. We've been told that the water level in Florida Bay can change as much as a foot, independent of tides, during prolonged northers.

Listen to locals, get good chart and weather information, and trust your own common sense.

Boating with the Big Boys

Some of the best boat-camping waters are those we must share with commercial vessels. Here, from the American Waterways Operators Foundation, are some tips to help keep you from tangling in a no-win situation with a tug or barge.

- Don't go boating when you're drinking or on drugs.

- Day or night, designate a lookout for commercial traffic.

- Know the rules for visibility and abide by them, especially at night. Thinking they were passing safely behind one ship and ahead of another, two young men hit a tow cable at high speed a few years ago. One died. Yet both ships were clearly marked with light signals that indicated one was under tow.

- Never pass close behind a tugboat, night or day. The tow cable could be submerged.

- Avoid sailing in commercial waters. Winds are always quirky at best, and a big ship could blank your breeze just when you most need steerage.

- If you're unsure of your situation or a commercial vessel's intentions, communicate with it on VHF channel 16 or 13.

- When a towboat or a barge is approaching a bridge or lock, it must line up with the opening well in advance, Once it is committed, changing course can be dangerous and difficult. You should stay out of the way.

- Don't water-ski or jet ski around big ships. Jumping the wakes can be thrilling; getting sucked through a propeller is less so.

- Avoid ship channels where possible.

- A series of short whistle blasts—five or more—signals danger.

- Use safe anchorages. It's illegal to tie up to navigation aids.

- Stay clear of cargo-loading docks and moored barges.

- "Wheel wash" can be very strong, even hundreds of yards behind a vessel. Extreme turbulence results.

- In narrow canals, be aware that the powerful engines of a tugboat or a towboat can suck a smaller vessel alongside. Don't try to pass in narrow waterways.

- Learn navigation rules and live by them.

11
Just for the Health of It

We once interviewed the most successful boat salesperson in town. She was a young mother who had found that one of the biggest reasons why families drew back from buying a boat was the mothers' fear for their children's safety. By stressing the safety and family fun of boating and by talking about her own boating experiences with her two preschoolers, she made sale after sale.

Ironically, boating's biggest risks can be dealt with quite simply: wear PFDs, check the weather, file a float plan, and observe the most obvious boating precautions. It's the nonmarine problems that can cause the most discomfort in boat camping.

Bugs and Such

Mosquitoes

Mosquitoes have murdered more mariners than all the muskets in history. Although some waterways are virtually mosquito free thanks to dam-controlled water levels that don't give them a place to breed, mosquitoes are an almost constant scourge. We have fought them in the Arctic, where they can survive a season frozen in solid ice, and in the tropics, when we were anchored on shoals two miles from the nearest land. On a summer morning in the Everglades mosquitoes are so thick you can kill an entire squadron with one swat.

As the kids would say, mosquitoes suck. According to the Tender Corporation, makers of a variety of bug fighters and treatments, there are about 200 species of mosquitoes in North America alone and 2,400 varieties worldwide. They can carry a long list of diseases, including malaria and encephalitis.

After more than forty years of trying to eradicate mosquitoes, the World Health Organization has thrown in the towel. Its strategy now is to educate people in preventing bites: cover the skin with clothing, with repellent, or with both. DEET, which was introduced during World War II, is the most effective and safe deterrent to date. It's available in many strengths and forms, from 100 percent DEET in an oily base to pleasant, light lotions.

There are two ways to avoid mosquito bites: keep them from getting at you and make yourself so distasteful they won't bite those spots they *can* get at.

Start by utilizing whatever screening will work in your particular boat-camping situation. Tents and other shelters should provide a total seal around you; any vents or openings, such as Dorade boxes, should be screened. Netting can be bought by the yard, carried in very little space, and draped each night over openings you can't close any other way.

Cover exposed skin with the repellent of your choice. We usually carry several types, ranging from the very concentrated Ben's Max to a natural, citronella-based repellent such as Natrapel. We don't know if it's our own chemistry, the setting, or the mosquitoes, but sprays work with different degrees of success at different times.

For the most extreme situations a body suit called Bug Armor is made by the Tender Corporation, Littleton, New Hampshire 03561 (603–444–5464). The suit consists of a hooded zipper-front jacket and drawstring trousers with elastic at the ankles. Lightweight mesh, it can treated with Ben's Max and worn over your regular clothes and headgear. A hat with mosquito netting that covers face and neck is available from the Vermont Country Store, Box 3000, Manchester Center, Vermont 05255 (catalogs are free).

Malaria isn't common in the United States, but if you're boat camping in infested areas, prophylaxis must be started before you go and continued after you get home. Check with your doctor for the latest drugs. Once infected, you'll probably be stuck with malaria for life, so taking the pills is a wise precaution.

No-See-Ums

The chief difference between these tiny, almost invisible biters and most other bugs is that they can fly through screens. We've been tormented by them on coasts from Nova Scotia to Central America. The itch is formidable. At first they raised watery blisters, and their scars lasted for weeks. In time we built up an immunity to them, but the symptoms recurred when we tangled with the no-see-ums of New Zealand. They must have been a different type.

If no-see-ums are a problem where you boat camp, try several repellents. We have no luck with mosquito sprays, but we do with an Avon bath oil called Skin-So-Soft. Although it's considered a folk remedy that has never been tested scientifically, it has been a lifesaver for us at times. A primitive, native repellent for no-see-ums is coconut oil.

Ticks

Ticks have been widely publicized since Lyme disease came into the picture, but they can vector a long list of other diseases too, some of which are fatal. Like mosquitoes, ticks tend to be thickest in the moist lowlands where most of us do our boat camping.

Flies

Some 60,000 types exist, ranging from the merely pesky to vicious biters that take a big chunk out of your hide. Once, when we were camping in Australia, we were swarmed by black clouds of harmless but maddening houseflies. Another time, as we sailed into Treasure Cay in the Bahamas, we were suddenly greeted by thousands of flies that filled our boat's cabin. Even when they aren't the biting variety, flies spread disease by landing on all sorts of unspeakable surfaces on their way to your potato salad.

The worst biting flies we've ever encountered were in the Bahamas, especially Andros, and in lake camping in Michigan.

Again, it pays to carry more than one repellent. What works on some flies doesn't work on others; and repellents that work for some people won't work for others. A folk remedy used by a Minnesota family is made by pouring the following ingredients into a one-quart spray bottle:

2 cups white vinegar
1 cup Avon Skin-So-Soft
1 tablespoon eucalyptus oil (from a health-food store)
Water, to fill the bottle.

The family use this spray several times a day on themselves and on their pets, and they swear it works against ticks, biting flies, and other pests.

Ants

More than mere picnic pests, ants have become a major threat now that fire ants have spread northward through the South and Southwest. Each year, according to the Tender Corporation, three to five million Americans are bitten by fire ants. Of the victims, 85,000 require medical treatment and as many as 30 die.

The boat camper's chief defense is to recognize the distinctive conical mounds built by fire ants and to stay well away from them.

Most of the more benign ants can be discouraged with commercial preparations. We've also had good luck with two homemade remedies. One is to mix equal parts of sugar and borax powder (it's found in supermarkets with laundry soaps). Dip wet sponges into the mixture and leave them along the pathways ants have been using to invade you.

Although you can buy sticky substances to "fence off" areas from the march of ants, we've jury-rigged our own by putting rings of tape, sticky side out, around dock lines. The first ants get stuck; succeeding waves turn back. Almost any sticky tape will do—duct, cellophane, electrical, or whatever else you have.

Chiggers

Generally, the same battle lines that apply for ticks and fleas are also effective for chiggers. Unlike those biters and suckers that go for open spaces on the skin, chiggers prefer to burrow under tight-fitting clothing, such as waistbands or sock tops. Clothing sprays coupled with skin sprays provide the best armor.

The Stings and Arrows of Sea Life

Fire coral, jellyfish, Portuguese man-of-war, and sea nettles are the major dangers encountered along the seashore. In the tropics sea urchins are also a danger. They look like pincushions, and their barbs are almost impossible to pull out.

By keeping your eyes open and watching where you put your hands or feet you can avoid fire coral and sea urchins. Floating hazards are harder to avoid. Man-of-war tentacles can waft as much as 50 feet under and around the floating "blue bottle." Give them a wide berth. Don't touch any you find along the beach, either: the venom lasts long after the creature itself has died.

Reactions vary, depending on your personal chemistry and the site and size of the sting or bite. Most of us get only a mild reaction, with itching, burning, and redness. A severe allergic reaction can cause pain over a wide area, muscle cramps, convulsions, and even respiratory paralysis. Any unusual reaction calls for immediate medical attention.

The first treatment, says the Tender Corporation, is to cleanse the bite and remove anything left in the wound. Toxins can continue to sting for up to an hour after they've been separated from their body. Use a scraping motion; squeezing just releases more poison into the wound. Along the Florida coast, some swimmers carry disposable safety razors and shave their legs after they tangle with a man-of-war.

The next step is to apply alcohol, ammonia, or a commercial compound, such as After Bite.

General Bug Strategies

In addition to applying repellents to your skin and clothing, using screens and netting, and deploying whatever air sprays or treatments you find useful (Yard Guard, citronella candles, punk coils), try to stay out of areas where bugs are worst *when* they are worst. The breezeless hours of early morning and early evening are choice times for mosquitoes and no-see-ums. When winds freshen, no-see-ums disappear almost completely. Flies become less active in cold weather.

Don't wear perfumes or use scented soaps. They attract most of the usual bugs, plus bees that otherwise wouldn't have much interest in you. According to the Tender Corporation, light-colored clothes attract bugs; darker shades are better.

Among the environmentally safe products you might carry with you are flypaper, borax laundry powder (against roaches as well as ants), and any traps you can buy or devise.

Here's a trap that catches a variety of light-loving bugs and is especially good for fleas. Partially fill an aluminum pie plate with water and add a drop or two of detergent to break the surface tension. Place the plate on the ground near the edge of the campsite, in the dark. Carefully place a votive candle in the water and light it. Fleas—which can leap 150 times the length of their own bodies and

---

In Praise of Nylon Net

Real mosquito netting can sometimes be found in outdoor-supply stores, army-surplus outlets, and catalogs. Cheesecloth drapes well, is tightly woven, and is extremely lightweight, but it tears so easily that it can almost be considered disposable.

For low cost, durability, and versatility, another choice is nylon net—the kind sold in fabric stores for making tutus. Ten yards of nylon net can be rolled up and crammed into a stuff bag smaller than a loaf of bread, and it can be used for many boat-camping chores. It costs less than a dollar a yard.

Use lengths of nylon net as mosquito draping over bunks or sleeping bags. Drape it over hatches and companionways to keep bugs out while letting breezes through. Use lengths of it as a strainer, a fishnet, or a colander.

As a dish scrubber, net digs out the goo but doesn't scratch plastic dishes or nonstick pans. When the dishes are done, shake out the net and put it away dry. It won't mildew or sour.

---

can lie in wait for you for as long as three months—jump for the glitter of the flame in the shiny pan but drown in the water. If you forget to snuff the candle, it puts itself out when it burns down to the water. We've caught hundreds of fleas a night this way, and the "trap" can be reused time and again.

Sun

Only in recent years has sunlight become known as the harsh destroyer that it is. Combine the sun's rays with reflections off a shiny boat and the surface of the water and the problem is compounded for today's boat campers.

Now we choose our sun hats for protection, not fashion, and there's always at least one spare aboard in case one gets lost. We like a sun hat that has a wide, all-around brim, such as the popular Tilley hat, or the Keys fisherman style, which has a flap to cover the back of the neck. And we're careful about sunglasses.

Sun blocks and lip balms go on well before 10:00 A.M., even on cloudy days. When we're likely to get wet we use only waterproof sun blocks. Read labels: some require several applications; some do not protect against both kinds of ultraviolet rays.

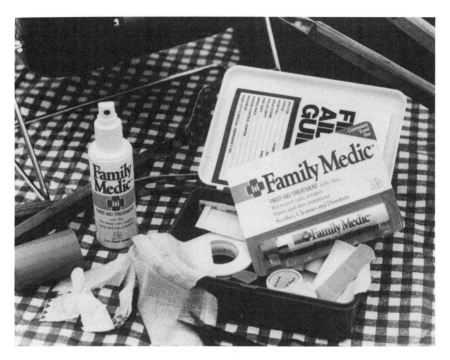

Start with a commercial first-aid kit, then add items specific to your trip and your family's medical needs. *Tender Corporation*

When snorkeling in clear, shallow waters swimmers burn quickly even underwater. It's a good idea to wear waterproof sun block, long-sleeved, lightweight pajamas, and a pair of socks. Cover-ups are the rule, preferably in sturdy but cool cottons. Most fabrics allow at least some ultraviolet rays to get through; thin synthetics offer almost no protection.

It's easy to carry a few sun flies in various sizes, with several hanks of light line for tying them to whatever trees, shrubs, or rigging can be found. Simply hem up scraps of canvas or sailcloth and place a stainless-steel or brass grommet in each corner. Easily tied in place, the shades can be moved, re-angled, or adjusted as the sun moves.

Such tarps do double duty. If they're also waterproof they can be used as ground cloths or dodgers or rigged as rain shields over tents, gear, or the outdoor kitchen. If they're strong enough they can also be used, sling style, for hanging food supplies in a tree where they're

safe from animals, as a hammock, or for hoisting an injured or
exhausted swimmer aboard.

Seasickness

Even the most iron-gutted sailor can get queasy. Scopolamine
patches, worn behind the ear, are very popular, and some people
also have good luck with pressure-point wristlets. Over-the-counter
seasick pills are oldies but goodies. Other people swear by such folk
remedies as ginger, saltines, or bouillon or by rituals such as putting
a dab of Vicks VapoRub in their navel.

Potions, patches, and pills should be chosen by you and your
doctor. Whether to eat or not eat is also a personal decision: a meal
that one person keeps down will send another person lurching for
the nearest bucket. Some practices, however, are a must:

- Get plenty of fresh air at all times. Forget the privacy of the cabin;
  use the lee rail.

- Watch the horizon, a cloud, the shoreline, or something else that
  doesn't move. Take the helm if possible. Pick a fixed point, not
  the compass, and steer on it.

- If you've ever been seasick, you know it can happen again, so
  don't wait for nausea to strike. Take medication before you leave
  port. Once you begin to vomit, it's too late.

Let's Play Doctor

In a small first-aid kit you might carry: self-stick pressure wrap,
gauze, and bandages of various sizes and types; moleskin (a lifesaver
for sore feet); a forehead thermometer; tweezers; safety pins; electrolyte tablets for heat stroke; triple antibiotic ointment; a pain
reliever; antiseptic; a first-aid manual; and any special medications
that a family member might need (such as an anaphylactic shock
kit or aspirin-free remedies).

For flyweight boat camping, Sawyer makes a first-aid packet that
is worn on the belt. It weighs only a few ounces, yet it contains a
wealth of help: adhesive wrap; bandages and gauze pads; antisep-
tics; antibiotic ointment; electrolyte tablets; pain pills; and a first-aid
manual with state-by-state emergency phone numbers.

If you assemble your own first-aid kit, carry all the conventional
items—scissors, bandages, tapes, anti-itch treatment, antibiotic

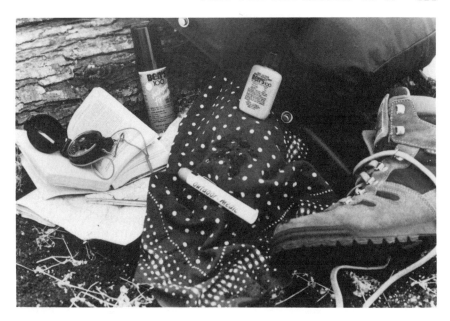

For flyweight boat camping, look for pocket- or sample-sized first-aid items that are sold in sporting-goods departments. *Tender Corporation*

ointment, pain pills, and the like—plus the best outdoor first-aid manual you have room for. Also useful are:

- Medical insurance-policy information.

- Telephone numbers for your doctors, dentists, and druggists.

- Written prescriptions, preferably by generic name. You can't always get refills in another state, but if you can provide the telephone numbers of your doctor and hometown druggist, it's likely that a pharmacist will be able to help you.

- A small, inexpensive magnifying glass, invaluable if you have to remove a sliver, a fishhook, or a tick, and to read the fine print on a container of medicine.

- Disposable heat and ice packs that can be activated as needed.

- Elastic bandages.

- Sample sizes of over-the-counter medications for diarrhea, constipation, motion sickness, pain, heartburn, colds, and coughs. They take up little room but give you a wide variety of treatments for unexpected ills.

- Antifungal powder in case someone picks up athlete's foot.

- A small tube of topical anesthetic for oral use (cankers, sore gums).

- Petroleum jelly to soothe dry, cracked, or chapped skin.

- Artificial tears to flush out eyes.

- Ipecac syrup, if your pediatrician recommends it. Make sure, however, that you know which toxins do *not* call for induced vomiting.

- A penlight. Even though each person aboard should have a personal light, it's handy to have a penlight that stays in the medical kit.

12
Kids on Board

Some of the happiest children we've ever known were boat babies. At night they were rocked to the lullaby of wavelets slapping against the hull. By day they bustled about their chores, earning as a reward the right to take the wheel. We knew one family of live-aboards whose children began to stand watch at the age of eight.

Kids on board learn responsibility, obedience, respect for nature, and a long list of skills from fishing to foraging, from navigation to knot tying. "Flemishing" the dock lines into flat coils became a passion for two eight-year-olds we had with us on different cruises. Another young crewmember fished for hours on end.

Although we've known children of all ages, from infants through teenagers, who lived full time on boats, it seems to us that the best boat-camping ages are from infancy until kids start to walk and from age four or five through the teen years. Toddlers aged one to three can be managed in boat camping too—as long as parents schedule most of their boating during nap time and are willing to chase, corral, and entertain their little ones constantly in camp. Toddlers are too old to sleep all day and too young to participate actively in the trip, so we rarely meet them on the trail.

Kid Stuff

The first rule of boating is to wear a PFD. If you choose a life jacket that fits your child comfortably (many do not) and treat it like a privilege instead of a punishment, you've won the battle. We know one family that keeps its life vests in their car, not on their boat. The

In boat camping there are chores for everyone. Children learn skills, responsibility, and resourcefulness. *Rubbermaid*

kids put them on in the car at the launch ramp and don't take them off until they're safely back in the car.

In boat camping you can't relax just because the boat is on the beach or at the dock. Where there's water, there's danger for little ones. Once, when we were cruising in the tropics, we met a family whose cute little girls were oblivious to the fact that they were wearing nothing *but* their weathered life vests!

Assuming your children wear more than life jackets, take twice as many clothes for them as you do for grown-ups—children get dirtier, colder, wetter, and sweatier. Include at least one extra pair of shoes, so one pair can be drying at all times. Take plenty of layers; taking a sweater off is much easier than wrestling a child out of a sweatshirt and into a T-shirt. In a pitching boat, changing clothes is next to impossible.

Get really good, tie-on safari sun hats that shade the eyes, ears, and back of the neck. Sunglasses are a plus if your child is old enough to wear them. Use plenty of high-SPF, waterproof sunscreens. We know now that sun damage is cumulative and irre-

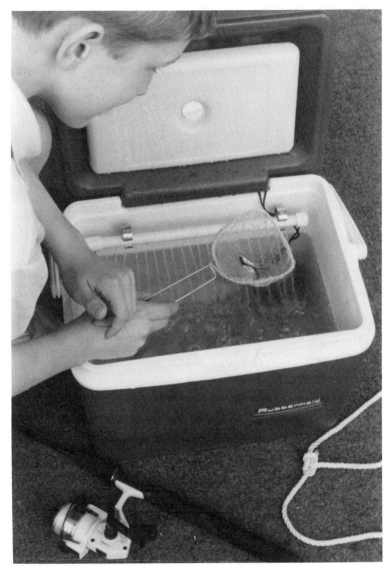

Where there's a boat, there's endless fun for kids. *Rubbermaid*

Make sure little ones get plenty of liquids, especially if they aren't yet able to ask for water. *Rubbermaid*

versible. As a doctor once said, "Your body never forgets a sunburn!" Young children have a long, sunny life ahead; start them young on good sunscreening habits.

Children get hungry and thirsty more often than adults do. Juices, even those that are 100 percent pure fruit juice, are sticky-sweet, so it's better to offer water. A pediatrician once told us that dehydration can be a real problem at the beach, especially in children who aren't able to talk and can't ask for water. Be liberal with liquids.

For snacking, have plenty of fruit or carrot sticks on hand. Individually wrapped lunch-box treats are portion controlled and are easier to serve on the go. Focus on healthful choices, such as plain popcorn, graham crackers or animal crackers, and individually boxed, low-sugar cereals, such as oat rings or bite-sized shredded wheat. Lightly salted popcorn also helps to prevent motion sickness in some children.

With children aboard, plan shorter hops. Stop often for playtime, potty time, and sightseeing even if there's nothing to sightsee. Make it an adventure by looking for four-leaf clovers, seashells, or doubloons. Have a separate activity bag for each child, choosing toys that are suitable both under way and in camp. Don't stuff it so full that there isn't room for souvenirs: smooth stones, shells, arrowheads, nuggets of driftwood.

The new *Peterson First Guide* Series, published by Houghton Mifflin, are packed with information. Pocket sized, they are color-illustrated, simplified field guides that adults and children alike will find invaluable. The series includes guides to astronomy, birds, caterpillars, clouds and weather, fish, insects, mammals, reptiles, rocks and minerals, seashores, shells, trees, and wildflowers. Carry as many as you have room for, and they'll pay for themselves time and again. Marlor Press publishes delightful vacation logbooks, nature notebooks, and diaries that supply blanks and questions to help the child write an account of a trip. Look for them in bookstores.

Milton Bradley makes a very good line of board games in travel sizes. If any of your games have magnetic pieces, though, be sure to keep them away from your compass. Playing cards are pure gold; they provide hours of fun and take up almost no space.

An excellent source of children's storybooks is the National Association for the Preservation and Perpetuation of Storytelling. Request a catalog from NAPPS, Box 309, Jonesboro, Tennessee 37659 (800–525–4514). The accent is on stories: soothing yarns for

Camping Games

"Trashure" hunt. This game can be played by one child alone or by any number of children and adults. The idea is to police up the campground and leave it cleaner than you found it.

One method is to give out a list of things to find: a pull-top, a Coke bottle, something that is used in the hair, a Snickers wrapper, and so on. The person who finds the most items on the list wins.

We find the game is just as much fun and results in a more thorough cleanup if everyone is given a trash bag with instructions to pick up every bit of litter that can be found. (We assume you've warned your kids not to pick up things they shouldn't touch.) In an envelope—which you can prepare before you leave home—seal a piece of paper on which you have written the item or items that will count toward first prize. When everyone gets back to camp with bulging bags, the envelope is opened and the contest begins. The "secret word" might be plastic six-pack holders, gum wrappers, things that are yellow, aluminum cans, peanut shells, or anything that's likely to be found in the area where you're camping. The person with the greatest number of the item(s) on the list wins.

Talent show. Everyone must sing a song, recite a poem, or tell a joke or story.

Radio show. For this you'll need an audio cassette recorder. Make a few copies of a suitable short play or skit. Assign roles and sound effects, and record your own radio drama. Rehearsing, performing, and listening to it will bring hours of hilarious fun. If you're holed up on a rainy day, this can be a lifesaver.

School. Everyone takes a turn at being the teacher. Mom and Dad might teach an "oldies" song, a limerick, a knot, or how to sew on a button. Older children can teach an algebraic formula or a French verb declension. Younger children can teach everyone a song, poem, or story they've learned in school. Everyone gets a chance to shine in a favorite subject.

Bean-bag toss. Seal up a cupful of dried beans in a zip-top sandwich bag, and then in a second bag for extra protection. Draw a circle in the dirt with a stick, and see how many times you can hit the bull's-eye. The beans serve as spare provisions.

Entertainment Afloat

License lotto. *This only works on waterways where you see a great many boats, of course. Mom, Dad, or an older child writes down a three-number combination. The first player to see that sequence of numbers in the license of a passing boat wins.*

Bingo. *Mom or Dad lists 10 or 15 items for each child to spot: specific varieties of birds or trees, a red barn, a house with a green door, an aluminum canoe, a boater wearing an orange life vest, a cloud with a silver lining, a floating leaf, a jumping fish, a boat with a Bimini top, and so on, according to the type of waters you're sailing. The first person to check off every item wins.*

Mark Twain. *A child with a sounding line can be put to work calling out depths every five minutes or so. (Don't play this on powerboats: the line could get caught in the propeller!)*

Nature diary. *Each child chooses a category, such as birds, trees, fish, wildflowers, clouds, butterflies, rocks and minerals, or something else you're likely to see throughout the cruise. Plan this game in advance so you can provide each child with a nature guide in his or her chosen category. Each time a specimen is sighted and positively identified, it is listed in the notebook or diary.*

I Spy a Spinnaker. *A variation on I Spy, this is a word game in which things in or on the boat are named. The first player calls out, "I spy a spinnaker," or any other item on the boat. The second player must "spy" something on the boat that begins with the last letter of the previous word—in this case, r—so he or she calls out, "I spy an RDF." The next player finds a word that begins with an f, and so on. No fair repeating, or naming items that aren't on the boat.*

Cruise to Cairo. *It's fun to see how long you can keep up a story in which all of the words start with the same letter. The first person begins the story by saying, "I took a cruise to Cairo." The second says, "I took a cruise to Cairo and cooked a chicken." The next player must add two more words starting with the letter c, such as "I took a cruise to Cairo and cooked a chicken that was colorful and crooked." The next, "I took a cruise to Cairo and cooked a crooked, colorful chicken named Carol Conners." When that one runs out of steam, try starting with "I sailed to Singapore," "I rowed to Rio de Janeiro," or "I paddled to Paducah." The longer and more outrageous the stories, the more fun everyone has.*

bedtime, scary tales to tell around the campfire, and audiotapes to listen to on rainy nights in the tent.

Tapes are perfect entertainers for children. By the time they're 12, you can hardly pry the earphones off their heads. A great many good songs and stories are available on tape for all ages. For children aged three to eight we recommend *Grandpa Wes' Nature Notebooks*. Read in a soothing, very gentle tone by educator and retired environmental engineer Wes Kunkel, the tapes are gems of entertainment—and each carries a science message as well. Write to Kunkel Artistic Technologies, Box 156, Richland, Washington 99352–0156.

Grandpa Art (Arthur Custer) sings about birds, insects, and other friends of nature. An award-winning musician who has written for *Sesame Street*, Custer creates delightful tapes that soon have children singing along. For information call 800–227–2712 or write to the Sun Group, 1133 Broadway, Suite 1527, New York, New York 10010.

Educational audiotapes also have a place in family camping and boating. There's almost always a time during the trip when everyone can tune in to French lessons or a course in music history. Audio Forum, best known for its extensive line of language-instruction tapes for adults and children, now offers tapes in Native American languages, including Cherokee, Choctaw, Kiowa, Mohawk, and Tlingit—at this writing, 10 in all. Learning one of them brings a special magic to a boat-camping trip, especially if you're learning a language that was spoken centuries ago on the very waters where you're boating.

Audio Forum offers hundreds of tapes: books on tape, courses, inspiration, music for fitness walkers, and much more. To order a free Audio Forum catalog, call 800–243–1234.

Better Safe Than Sorry

Sturdy netting is used on sailboats to fill in lifelines so small children can't slip through. Net can also be used to make a bunk into a playpen or to close a hatch or a companionway that a child might fall through or crawl through. By making your own netting you can have as much as you want, where you want it.

However, if you prefer a removable net, look for Cargo Marine Net in stores or write to CJV Associates, 2500 West Higgins Road, Hoffman Estates, Illinois 60195. In a kit you'll receive a 29-inch length (stretchable to 34 inches) of ultraviolet-stabilized, polyester net, plus four hooks. Peel off the backing and stick the hooks anywhere in the boat. Thanks to 3M's very high bond (VHB) adhesive, they'll grip like barnacles. The high-quality, ultraviolet-resistant cargo net is perfect for storage areas, and it can also turn a quarter-berth or a forepeak into a playpen. It's easily hung up and taken down as needed.

As soon as children are old enough, make them a part of every safety plan and drill. The 911 emergency telephone system has proved that children as young as age two can be lifesavers. In boating, children can be taught, depending on their ages and abilities, to make a Mayday call, use a fire extinguisher, throw a line and monkey fist, or toss an MOB marker.

Because one of the cardinal safety rules of both boating and camping is to know where you are, map and chart reading can be taught at a child's skill level. Younger kids can be taught about strobe lights, flashlights, and chemical light sticks. Older kids can learn to use flares and a CB radio.

Have safety drills on board, with a job for each child even if it's something as simple as "Duck!" which will come in handy in an all-standing jibe. Practice responding to other orders, too. When children hear "Fist!" they must make fists before the boat rams the dock or before a hatch flips over, so their fingers can't get caught. When "Brace!" is barked children must hang on however they can, to protect themselves in an unexpected grounding or an imminent collision.

One of our drills is "Jump!" It's an extreme measure, but it paid off once just before we were rammed at a dock. In that case we only had to jump from the boat to the dock, but in a fire or an explosion you may want your family to jump overboard immediately, with no questions asked. New drills may have to be added for special situations, such as locking or rafting up.

In the navies and merchant ships of the world, the buck stops with the captain. It's a good practice in family boating and camping, too. We've all heard stories about tragedies that occurred when each parent thought the other one was watching the children. No matter how calm the day, how short the voyage, or how seemingly safe the campsite, adults must "hand over the watch," so that someone is always aware of what's going on and of who's in command of what.

Schoolchildren are accustomed to fire drills, and you've probably held family drills at home. So your children should be quick studies on the subject of boat-camping fire drills. Most of the familiar safety rules apply:

- Don't enter a fire to save anything, not even your best doll.

- Stay together; look out for each other. At each campsite agree on a family gathering spot, such as in front of the latrines, in case a fire breaks out in the tent or on the boat. In an emergency, precious time can be lost while family members look for each other. With a designated rallying point, everyone knows where to go.

- If your clothes catch fire, Stop, Drop, and Roll.

- If a police officer, a Coast Guard officer, a forest ranger, or a fire fighter gives you an order, obey even if you're afraid.

- Never jump into the water to save someone. Instead, yell for grown-ups while you toss a line or a life ring.

- Know your address. This rule gets complicated in boat camping, when your "address" has no street number and changes every day. However, in campsites where a telephone is available, it takes only a few minutes to hold a family powwow to talk about where you are ("Lakeview State Park, Site 32," for example). In areas without telephones, a brief family discussion can establish a reasonably accurate location (such as "the north side of the river, three miles west of Rivertown"), in case a radio call must be made.

13
Cooking Afloat and Ashore

One of the greatest pleasures of boat camping is cooking and eating. Even with the smallest boat you can escape the crowds and find your own private cove or beach for a picnic or a campfire. If solitude means more to you than the convenience of a public campsite with running water, a grill, and a big picnic table, your boat can always take you to places where others won't (or can't) follow.

Our list of memorable camp meals goes back through the years. We remember sandy beaches on deserted islands in the tropics, in the shade of casuarina trees—they're called singing pines for good reason. We remember pebbled shores along cold, clear northern lakes and rocking at anchor in rivers as we spread out a picnic lunch on the seat of a canoe or john boat. Once, in a TVA lake, we nudged our pontoon boat ashore under a canopy formed by a fragrant mimosa tree, miles from anyone else, and dug into sandwiches and salads.

At times you may envy the yachtie with the big, luxurious galley and kitchen conveniences, but let's list the joys of having a portable galley. While that yachtie is stuck with one galley, yours can offer a new layout and a new view every day. Set it up in sun or in shade, in the open or under a shelter, on the dock or the beach or the riverbank, or in your waterfront campsite with its electrical outlet and running water.

When you're boat camping in a very small boat all cooking must be done ashore, but we've also boat camped aboard boats that had enough room on deck or in the cockpit to set up a stove and galley so we could stay out "on the hook."

Stoves are available in sizes to suit every boat camper, from a kayak backpacker to a big-boat camper. *Peak 1*

There's nothing like waking up at anchor, afloat on a mirrored lake, your boat wrapped in its own cotton-candy mist, and starting the coffee on deck as you watch the early cat's-paws gently stroke the fog away.

The Stove

Even if you're determined to do all your cooking over campfires, it's essential to have a small stove of some kind to use on rainy days and where open fires are not permitted. Fire bans are becoming more common, even in the most remote wilderness, and sometimes you don't know about them until you arrive. Trust us. Bring a stove, even if it's only a pocket stove, and a supply of whatever fuel it uses.

Camp stoves come in dozens of sizes, models, and weights and with a choice of many fuels. The classic Coleman gasoline stove has

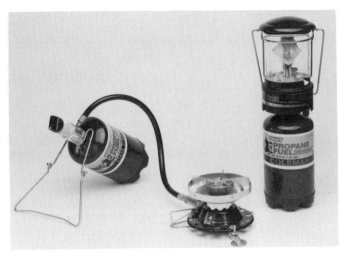

Peak 1's propane stove and lantern. *Peak 1*

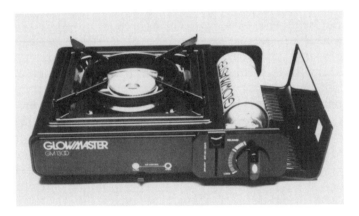

Small butane buffet burners go anywhere. Fuel canisters are disposable. *National Marine Products*

proved itself in the wilderness for decades and is sure to be the choice of many boat campers. We've had hours of use from a lightweight single-burner model, and we've cooked entire banquets on the two-burner "suitcase" type. Coleman now makes a three-burner gas camp stove, the ultimate luxury.

For flyweight boat camping, look at the Peak 1 line of backpack stoves. The line includes the new Apex component stoves, which combine a burner with a hose that hooks up to a cylinder filled with Coleman fuel or kerosene. Fuel feed is automatic, and no priming cup is needed. The entire system weighs just over a pound. Peak 1 also offers featherweight multifuel models with built-in tanks for Coleman fuel or kerosene. Optimus and Primus are also well-known, time-proved names in camp stoves.

Coleman fuel is a very hot, clean-burning, easy-to-light fuel that gives lots of BTUs per pound, per dollar, and per gallon. In some ways it's more dangerous to use in a boat than kerosene or alcohol, but boat campers who use outboard motors are well practiced in working safely with gasoline.

Propane and butane are also very hot, efficient fuels. The gas can be lit instantly without a match, by using a sparker, and the flame burns clean and blue, just like your gas stove at home. Gas cooks a meal in jig time. On the minus side, gas cartridges are costly, and most smaller types cannot be refilled. Empties must be packed out of the wilderness and disposed of properly. Some cartridges aren't recommended for saltwater boating because they could corrode quickly and let all of the propane leak into the bilges. And butane won't vaporize in very cold temperatures.

Kerosene is an inexpensive, hot-burning fuel that has always been one of our favorites, although it may be hard to come by in some boating areas. Ironically, it's easier to find in most Third World wildernesses than along many of America's busiest waterways.

Kerosene has taken a bad rap with some boaters because they've had nasty experiences with stinking, sooty, yellow kerosene flames. Good camp stoves solve the problem by using various preheating devices to deliver the kerosene to the burner as a gas, after which it burns blue, clean, and almost odor free. Properly used and maintained, a kerosene camp stove gives you all the convenience of propane at far less cost.

Although alcohol is still a common galley fuel, it's our last choice in fuels because it takes twice as much fuel, twice as long to cook a meal, to bring the teakettle to a boil, or to heat bathwater. It's an easy fuel to light, but the fumes are sharp and make your eyes smart. Two types of alcohol stoves are available: pressurized stoves, which are pumped up to force the fuel to the burner; and nonpressurized stoves, which may be considered somewhat safer but which also smell bad and cook slowly.

People who swear by such stoves point out that an alcohol fire can be put out with water. However, if you splash a bucket of water on a big pool of burning alcohol, it can just spread the burning fuel

The Sportsman's Oven has a shelf attached to its lid. It holds a standard 8-inch-square pan. *Fox Hill Corporation*

more widely. Because alcohol is so inefficient, you'll have to stow, tote, and dispose of twice as many jugs as you will for any other fuel. And alcohol costs much more than other fuels.

Combination alcohol-electric stoves are popular with boat cooks who prepare most of their meals while they are docked in marinas and plugged into shore power. However, they're not good portables. If you want to be able to cook with electricity when it is available, carry an electric coil heater, a small electric coffee pot or kettle, or an electric buffet burner.

Among other means of cooking you can use are:

Barbecues. Charcoal imparts a delicious taste, but it's bulky, inefficient, slow to start, and dangerous. Damp charcoal can ignite from spontaneous combustion. If you do carry charcoal aboard, keep it in a sealed metal container. Trendy new barbecues come along each year, using newspaper or some special solid fuel, but it's best to stick with stoves that have withstood the tests of time and hard use.

Electrical appliances. Portable, convenient 110-volt and 12-volt burners are available, and a full line of 12-volt coffee makers, toasters, electric skillets, and other appliances are offered by camping-supply stores. Consider them only if your boat-camping situation calls for them and only if you have plenty of surplus 12-volt juice. If you do carry electrical appliances, keep them cushioned and dry in their own protective bags. Without good care they'll rust away rapidly in saltwater boating.

Solar power. It's fun to use sun power as a supplemental cooker, but the sun has a way of hiding when you need it. Still, solar cookers are increasingly popular in the Third World, and new technology and materials make them more efficient and more portable than ever before. For full instructions on building and using solar cookers, buy *Cooking with the Sun*, published by Morning Sun Press, Box 413, Lafayette, California 94549.

Solid fuels. Sterno and other solid fuels are clean burning and convenient, but they have a fumy smell, fairly low BTU rating, and comparatively high cost. Still, a folding, pocket-sized solid-fuel stove can be a lifesaver as an emergency backup cooker.

Ice and Refrigeration

Even the smallest cruisers are now available with built-in 12-volt refrigerators and freezers. Portable 12-volt refrigerators are also available, to run off your boat or vehicle. Thermoelectric models can be reversed, to chill in one mode and to heat in the other. (In the heat mode they keep food warm; they aren't used for cooking.)

Still, these coolers are so small that you'll probably also need an ice chest or two. It's best to keep fish and bait in a cooler of their own because of the slime and smell. It's also wise to keep cold drinks in a separate cooler so the crew doesn't open and close the main icebox or refrigerator too often.

As a boat camper you have three basic choices. You can carry a combination of refrigeration and ice chests, ice chests alone, or neither. During the 10 years we lived aboard our small sloop in the Bahamas, we chose to go without any ice or refrigeration for months at a time.

The disadvantages of living without ice are obvious, but the hardships are fewer than most modern families expect. When you cruise without a cooler your only foods are those that are preserved or that can be harvested on the spot. Yet these can include a delicious variety of long-lasting fruits and vegetables: potatoes, nuts, apples, wild berries, and cascades of sprouts grown as you need them, as well as fresh fish, country hams, and hard cheeses.

Warm drinks are distasteful to the American palate at first, but even in the tropics we learned to enjoy drinks that were not iced. In exchange, we gained freedom from a thousand worries: Were we depleting the battery by running the refrigerator too long? Would we get food poisoning because the ice chest was too warm? Would we have to leave a rustic port before we were ready, only because the chicken was defrosting and we had to look for a new supply of ice? Could we trust the ice we were putting in our drinks? Who made it, and how safe was the water it was made from?

Ice has other drawbacks. In most boat camping—especially during loading, off-loading, and portages—ice is a heavy luxury. Water weighs eight pounds per gallon. Drainage from ice chests can be a smelly mess. If it collects in the bottom of a wooden boat, it can cause mildew and rot.

In the boondocks you can't always be choosy about ice. Cube ice hardly lasts overnight. Block ice may be rubbery soft. Dry ice is tricky to use and is not available in the wilderness.

Now that we live in a real house again we often make ice to carry along on one- or two-day boat-camping outings. Clean water, frozen in a clean container, will melt into drinkable water. We don't use eutectic "blue" ice units except on one-day trips. Once they thaw, they're just dead weight until you can freeze them again.

Sometimes, of course, nature provides all the chilling one needs. When you're boating in cold water, bottled drinks can be cooled by putting them overboard in a strong net bag. In very cold waters the bilge of the boat itself becomes a suitable chiller. And in areas where night temperatures go down to the 30s or low 40s, you can keep things cold simply by leaving the cooler lid open at night and closed during the day.

Even if you take some ice along as a luxury, it's best not to rely on it for foods that spoil quickly. High-risk foods, such as fresh meat and fish, mayonnaise salads, and milk products, have to be kept at 45° or below to inhibit the growth of harmful organisms.

If you have a refrigerator, keep a thermometer inside it to monitor the temperature. Most small refrigerators use an absorption system or a bimetallic unit. They aren't as efficient as the compressor type of refrigeration unit you have at home. They are slow to cool down and are difficult, and sometimes impossible on very hot days, to keep at safe temperatures.

We have several favorite coolers. For fly-in charters, when we must arrive in the islands with complete provisions for a week or two, we take one or two high-quality, insulated, soft-sided fabric coolers. Once the food or ice is gone or is stowed elsewhere, these well-insulated bags can be used as cushions or pillows. On the trip home they can be packed and checked as luggage.

Be sure to buy a cooler that is waterproof inside and out—in other words, a cooler that can sit in the wet without taking on water and in which ice can melt without leaking out. Ours, made by Cool Cat, have proved effective and durable over years of use.

We also have a large, hard-sided ice chest that is perfect for one- and two-day trips. We fill it at home with foods and homemade ice blocks, and off we go. The lid locks shut, so animals can't get into it at night. The chest floats, is waterproof, and has a textured, flat top that can serve as a seat, a work surface, or a dish drainer.

Incidentally, any ice chest will work far more efficiently for you if you prechill it with sacrificial ice the night before. In the morning dump out all of the water and old ice and refill the chest with fresh ice and with foods that have been prechilled or frozen.

We once talked to a sailor who carried enough fully cooked meals in ice chests for a 10-day Pacific passage. Every recipe was put into boilable bags, then frozen in boxes or molds so that they hardened in a boxy shape. This procedure not only saved space but also eliminated air spaces that would have hastened thawing. The blocks of frozen food were packed tightly into ice chests with dry ice; the chests were then labeled and taped shut. Packing and planning were done carefully, so that one chest was emptied before the next was opened. On the last day the remaining food was thawed but still cold.

Dry ice, by the way, "melts" into carbon dioxide, so don't sleep in a tightly closed boat in which dry ice is venting. Handle dry ice only with gloved hands, and wrap it in newspaper so it doesn't "burn" the food or the walls of the cooler.

Cooking Gear

All of us have our own definitions of basic necessity, luxury, and everything in between. One camp cook might never consider traveling without a potato peeler; another might never need anything more than a Swiss army knife. Because our own boat camping takes many forms, the list changes for each outing, depending on the size of the boat and the length and type of trip.

In flyweight camping by canoe or kayak, for example, one may be

Knives

The most indispensable tool in the outdoors life is a knife. The scuba diver is never without a knife in a sheath strapped to a leg; the sailor keeps a bosun's knife on the belt at all times; the angler has a favorite filleting knife; the hunter, a flaying knife. Knives are so important to chefs that they always travel with their own.

One of the most important decisions you'll make in boat camping will be in selecting the right knives for your type of boating, camping, cooking, fishing, and whatever outdoor hobbies you enjoy. For a lot of people one knife does everything, from whittling cooking utensils out of driftwood to trimming toenails.

Our minimum galley needs include a paring knife, a bread knife (because we eat a great deal of homemade bread), and a medium-sized butcher knife. If there is room we take more knives in different sizes, plus a vegetable peeler. For more about all-purpose knives and sharpening, see Chapter 7.

able to carry little more than aluminum foil and perhaps a pot for boiling water. In a larger boat that we can load while it's on the trailer at home, we may carry several big tote boxes filled with tableware, pots, dishes, and food.

It was once common for campers and boaters to build their own portable pantries, and we've seen some very clever ones made out of plywood. Today, however, so many featherweight aluminum "kitchens" are available that it's difficult to imagine a home design that would be better.

The Coleman Kitchen, for instance, is the size of a small suitcase. When it is set up it forms a work surface with storage shelves and hooks and a sink, plus an extension that is large enough to hold a two-burner camp stove. When the lid is closed it's a backgammon or checkers table. It can be set up freestanding or used without its legs atop a tailgate, deck, or picnic table. The whole affair weighs only 35 pounds.

Often we carry nothing more than a few heavy-duty plastic tote boxes, which double as seats and work surfaces wherever we are setting up the galley *du jour*. With their lock-on lids, these plastic boxes keep supplies safe from marauding wildlife. They're safe from rain and flooding too, and if we should capsize they might even float.

size from a shoe box to a treasure chest, and other brands can also be found in hardware and automotive stores. Look for heavy-duty plastics, not those that are designed for closet storage.

Many other multipurpose plastic carriers are available in discount and houseware stores. For special needs you might also find the right design in a bait shop, a tool department, or an auto-parts store. One of the ready-mades, such as a box designed to fit the bed of a pickup truck, might fit your needs exactly.

Have you found, as we often have, that many camp-cooking accessories look better than they actually work? It's fun to try folding table-and-chair sets, cute plastic sinks with a built-in water pump, and collapsible gazebos, but many such items are flimsy or impractical. This is one more area in which it's wise to get some camping experience before spending a fortune on gear that looks good in a catalog.

Cookware

In cookware, as in every other phase of boat camping, we recommend that you start simply and then build up your gear as you learn more about your boat, boat camping, and camp cooking. Most tyros start out in one of two ways: either they buy everything in the camping catalog, charge it to a credit card, and years later are still paying for stuff they never use; or they round up all the old kitchen castoffs they had banished to the basement or the garage and figure they're good enough for camping. Wrong on both counts.

We started with kitchen discards and garage-sale junk. Some of it worked flawlessly, but most of it was a lesson in exactly what we didn't want to carry with us. It's tough enough to cook in camp with good equipment, chosen for its specific purpose. To start out with things that don't work is to double your handicap.

Except for the very lightest, backpack-style boat camping, we don't like flimsy camp-cooking pots because they lose their heat rapidly on cold, windy days. We'd rather carry one or two heftier pots, with good lids. Here are our thoughts on cooking gear:

A cast-aluminum skillet with a cast lid. Brand names include Club Aluminum, Wearever, and Magnalite. A heavy skillet can be used as a griddle, skillet, roaster, or stove-top oven. Some of the best pizza, meat loaf, baked potatoes, and other favorites are made on top of the stove in such skillets.

Stacking cookware of high-quality stainless steel. It's costly, so don't invest in it unless you know what you want and take good

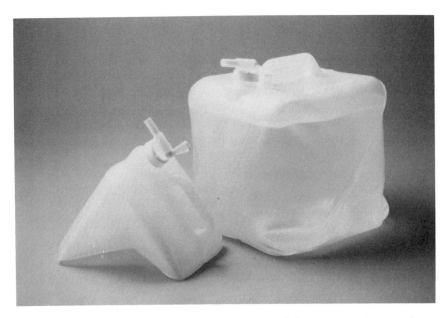

With a collapsible water jug you can have gravity-fed running water anywhere. *Rubbermaid*

care of it. If you do, it will last you for years. We have a pot/steamer/double-boiler set that does triple duty on one burner.

Ironware. Unlike many camp cooks, we are not devotees of cast-iron skillets. For boat camping they are double trouble because they're heavy and they rust. It's one thing to use an iron pot over a big campfire, but on a small camp stove or galley burner, iron pots develop hot spots over the flame. To spread the heat, old-time cooks used thick layers of grease. Most of us don't cook that way any more.

A pressure cooker. Although it's big and bulky, this is a very versatile pot that saves fuel and time. It you can have only one pot, take a pressure cooker. It can be used with or without pressure and, by using inserts, you can cook entire menus in it. We also use ours as a stove-top oven.

A stainless-steel bucket. It's an all-purpose utensil that can be used as a water heater, dishpan, lobster pot, water hauler, laundry basin, or cleaning bucket. Ours serves as a carryall in which we pack up all the galley odds and ends. It's the first thing we unpack when we make camp and the last thing we pack.

Nonstick pan(s). Choose a proven, name-brand, nonstick lining such as T-Fal, Resistal, or Silverstone, because some of the cheaper ones don't work. In most cases cleanup consists of nothing more than wiping the pan with a paper towel. Stacked with other pans or rattling around in your boat, these coated pans can be damaged. So stack them with dish towels to protect the coating, or, better still, sew a simple cotton cover to slip over each pan. Don't forget to take nylon utensils that won't scratch the pans.

Dishes. Sturdy, attractive plastic dishware is available in housewares, discount, and grocery stores. Rubbermaid makes a line of open-stock plastic dishware; buy only the pieces you need. Unbreakable Melamine dishes in nautical designs are sold in marine stores and catalogs. We've had years of service from our set of Yachting Tableware. Enamelware is campy looking and inexpensive, but it chips and eventually rusts. Stainless-steel mess kits are the right choice for many families. They are stackable, durable, and lightweight.

Silverware. In choosing utensils, look for clean styling. Despite its sporty good looks, we recommend against two-part silverware with plastic or wooden handles. In slapdash camp dishwashing, crevices or seams can trap food or soap scum.

Knives should be serrated so they can be used as steak knives as well as butter spreaders. Available in camping-supply stores are stainless-steel knife-fork-spoon sets that lock together. They are compact and practical, especially for single-handers.

Utensils. Most people who write books about boating and camping present you with a list of utensils. We suggest that you make your own list, with an emphasis on double and triple use for every inch and every ounce. Say, for example, that your galley will include a set of measuring cups. Plastic measuring cups are just that. They measure, period. However, long-handled, stainless-steel measuring cups can also be used as soup ladles or as miniature pans in which to melt butter or warm pancake syrup.

In addition to whatever spatulas, wooden spoons, knives, and other utensils you need, consider:

A double-geared can opener. Cheaper, single-gear types don't work as well on rusted or odd-shaped cans. The best choice for flyweight boat camping is the army-type folding-blade can opener. It's only as big as a thumbnail and, with patience and effort, will open any shape or size of can.

Collapsible water jugs. No matter how many other water carriers, built-in tanks, or jugs you have, we recommend carrying one or more of the collapsible type. When they're not in use they take up very little room. They weigh little, so they're the best type if you have to walk long distances in search of potable water to bring back to the boat or campsite. And they have built-in spigots, so you can have gravity-fed running water anywhere, anytime.

A *stove lighter.* Camp stores sell many types. Some produce a flame and are fueled by butane or lighter fluid. You'll need a flame lighter to start a campfire, charcoal, or a candle. Other types produce only a spark, to light a gaseous fuel. Among sparkers are models that use flints, batteries, or a piezo coil. We recommend a piezo coil because it has nothing that will wear out or need to be replaced.

A *thermometer.* As we've mentioned, the only way to be sure that the temperature inside your ice chest or refrigerator is within the range of safety is to keep an inexpensive refrigerator thermometer in it. If you can find one with a probe, you can see the temperature without opening the lid.

Foods for Boat Camping

It would make a strange menu, but you could probably live for months out of a backpack filled with rice, peanut butter, and dried apricots, assuming that drinkable water was also available. If you're boat camping on fly-sized space and weight allowances, you can do a great deal with powders, whole grains, concentrates, dried meats and hard sausages, and dehydrated foods.

The operative word here is foods. Where weight and space are pinched to the max, you can't afford to carry non-nutritive drink powders or sugary, empty-calorie desserts.

As space and weight allowances go up, so do dining pleasures. Add fresh fruits and vegetables, the best canned soups and stews, UHT milk, and the ultimate indulgence, ice. That, in turn, opens another cornucopia of possibilities: fresh meat for the grill, meals you've made at home, fresh milk and eggs, butter, and more.

Much of your meal planning will also depend on whether you must arrive at the boat with everything for a week in the wilderness, or whether you'll be shopping in local markets and eating an occasional restaurant meal.

In any case, Groene's Law calls for having extra provisions for at least one day. You can't count on making landfall when and where you planned, and you can't count on finding the stores open when you do. In other countries we're always being fooled by holidays and

Freeze-dried foods are expensive, and not everyone likes them, but they're hard to beat for flyweight boat camping. Read labels ahead of time: Some are eaten as is; others are eaten after water is added; still others must be cooked after rehydrating. *Gordon Groene*

business hours that are different from our own. Even in the American boondocks storekeepers tend to be rugged individualists who put up a Closed sign on the first day of the trout season or the bow-hunting season, on Sundays, or on any other day you're desperate for a bag of ice or a loaf of bread.

If everything goes perfectly and you have all those extra provisions left over at the end of the cruise, take them home or give them away. Nothing has been lost. Food is insurance—and an inexpensive policy, at that.

14
Meals on Keels

Boat camping—and boat campers—are so varied that no one recipe book can please us all. Our own boat camping ranges from inshore exploration along heavily populated rivers and canals, where we can dine in waterfront restaurants at least once a day, to weeks in the outback, where we have no refrigeration or opportunities to reprovision.

Most boat campers are probably somewhere between these two extremes. Usually we are able to reprovision at least occasionally and to have dinner ashore from time to time.

When you go boat camping, you may have ice always, occasionally, or never. You may be able to shop daily along the way. It's part of the fun, especially when you're in foreign countries. Or, you may have to leave home with the car, boat, or even a backpack filled with everything you'll need for a week or two.

Foraging for food is increasingly difficult because population pressures have forced the placing of Do Not Pick signs in even the most remote areas. Still, fishing can provide the mainstay of some boat-camping menus. Sometimes we have also lucked into an abundance of berries, fiddleheads, nuts, and other wild edibles.

Your gear may include a two-burner camp stove with a stove-top oven or a tiny backpack burner. Or you may rely completely on campfires and carry no stove at all. If you boat camp only in developed campsites you need carry little or no water. When you are boating the Keys, Baja, or the Bahamas, however, you must carry every drop of fresh water.

Start your own boat-camping cookbook by collecting recipes that work for your tastes, galley gear, cruising area, budget, and family needs. Collecting and experimenting with boat-camping recipes makes a good winter project. In fact, practicing at home is a must. Many dishes don't work out the way you planned. When a dish flops at home, you can always send out for pizza. Once you're in the wilderness, it's best to stick with tried-and-true recipes.

Before we moved aboard our tiny sloop to cruise the Bahamas without an oven for 10 years, Janet experimented for weeks with baking atop the stove, canning meats, and learning ways to keep yogurt and sourdough alive without refrigeration. The hard-won lessons learned ahead of time at home and in the early years on the boat really paid off.

Keeping in mind that all of us have different tastes, equipment, and boat-camping priorities, here are some one-burner recipes. Each makes about four servings.

Shrimp Corn Chowder

2 7-ounce cans shrimp	1 can evaporated skim milk
2 cans cream of corn soup	2 soup cans water
1 can cream of potato soup	Butter, thyme

Drain and rinse the shrimp. Combine the soups, milk, and water in a medium pot and heat gently, stirring until it's smooth and hot. Stir in the shrimp and heat until bubbles begin to form around the edges. Don't let it come to a boil. Put a pat of butter in each soup bowl, sprinkle it with thyme, and ladle in the soup.

Complete the meal with crisp pilot crackers and crunchy McIntosh apples for dessert.

Dishwashing: 1 soup pot, 1 bowl and 1 spoon per person.

Trash: 2 small cans, 4 medium-sized cans.

Special tip: Carry small amounts of herbs in plastic film canisters.

For more of Janet Groene's recipes, see her Cooking on the Go *(Hearst Marine Books) and* Cooking Aboard Your RV *(Ragged Mountain Press). The books can be ordered in any bookstore.*

More Tips from the Groene Galley

● *To make trash more compact, remove the labels and both ends of cans. Place the ends inside the cans, then flatten them. Labels can be burned if you have a campfire.*

● *You'll have no salad plates to wash if you serve crudités instead. Or marinate chunks of raw vegetables in Italian dressing, then thread them on skewers to make individual servings.*

● *If you start out with hard-frozen ground beef, it should keep for several days in a well-iced cooler. Double-wrap it so leaking juices can't contaminate the ice. Form it into burgers or meatballs in camp. Or cook and crumble the meat thoroughly at home, then drain and freeze it. Meats should be kept raw and cold or cooked and cold. Never cook meat partially with the intention of completing the cooking in camp. Partial cooking doesn't kill harmful bacteria; the heat hastens their growth.*

● *To avoid dishwashing, use edible dishes: avocado halves filled with chicken salad, cantaloupe halves piled high with cut-up fresh fruit or cottage cheese, green-pepper halves filled with ham salad, cored apples stuffed with peanut butter, scrambled eggs wrapped in big, warm, flour tortillas, and so on.*

● *Never throw away a jar that can be used as a shaker first. A little mayo left in the jar? Shake it up with half a dozen eggs and your favorite seasonings to make an omelet. A few peanuts left in the jar? Add two cups of milk and a package of instant pudding, shake, and pour into flat-bottomed ice-cream cones for an instant dessert. All the pickles gone? Use the remaining juice as part of the liquid in shaking up a salad-dressing mix.*

● *Buy bean salad, German potato salad, and mayonnaise-style potato salad in cans. If they need extra doctoring, add grated onion or sliced hard-boiled eggs.*

● *Scandinavian crispbreads such as Kavli or Wasa are a crisp, grainy, fiber-rich substitute for fresh bread. Unlike many other snack crackers, they're made with whole grains and contain little or no fat.*

Cook in foil and eat from the foil, and you won't have to wash dishes. *Gerber Products Company*

Fish Fry in Foil

4 teaspoons olive oil
4 meaty fish fillets
4 medium potatoes
4 medium onions

4 medium carrots
4 sun-dried tomatoes
Salt, pepper, thyme

Lay out four generous-sized squares of foil. On each, place a teaspoon of olive oil and a piece of fresh fish. Thinly slice the potatoes and carrots. Peel and thinly slice the onions. Layer the vegetables atop the fish and sprinkle with salt, pepper, and thyme. Form packets, using a double fold for all edges of the foil. Place on a grill over coals for about 15 minutes on each side. Time will vary according to the fire and the thickness of the fish.

The packets can also be baked over a burner in a clean, covered skillet. Test one packet for doneness after 25 minutes. If the packets have been well sealed, they won't leak. The skillet remains clean.

Open the packets carefully (there will be scalding steam) and eat directly from the foil.

Complete the meal with crusty rolls with squeeze margarine, individual cups of deli cole slaw, and Tootsie Pops for a walking dessert to enjoy as you take a sundown bird-watching hike.

Dishwashing: 1 paring knife, 4 forks.

Trash: 4 wads foil, deli containers, lollipop sticks.

Special tips: Scrub the potatoes and carrots before you leave home. Dry them well and wrap them individually in clean paper towels. This eliminates having to scrub them in camp, and the paper towels don't go to waste because you can reuse them. Shopping at the deli, buy a pound of cole slaw and ask that it be divided among four individual containers. Keep it on ice.

Tex-Mex Onedish

1 16-ounce can chili without beans
1 28-ounce can Mexican-style tomatoes

1 8-ounce can corn kernels
1 16-ounce can kidney beans
1 box cornbread mix
1 egg

Don't drain the vegetables. In a large skillet, mix the chili, tomatoes, corn, and kidney beans. Cover over low flame and bring

Bake a cornbread topping atop chili, and you have an entire meal in one dish.
Tabasco 7-Spice Chili

to a boil. Meanwhile, mix the cornbread mix, egg, and water as called for on the package in a plastic bag just until everything is evenly moistened. Strip the batter out of the bag onto the boiling chili. Cover and cook about 10 minutes or until the cornbread is firm and cooked through. Divide among four bowls.

Complete the meal with saltines, celery and carrot sticks, and one banana per person for dessert.

Dishwashing: 1 skillet, 1 serving spoon, 4 bowls, 4 spoons.

Trash: 4 cans, 1 burnable box, 1 plastic bag.

Special tips: Instead of carrying extra spices to give zest to this dish, buy the chili and the tomatoes preseasoned, in whatever heat your family likes. Prepare the celery and carrot sticks at home. Dry them well, bag them in plastic, and keep them on ice.

Hamburger Scramble

1 pound lean ground sirloin	1 tablespoon diced, dried green pepper
1 28-ounce can tomatoes	
1 cup uncooked rice	1 teaspoon chicken bouillon granules
3 tablespoons diced, dried onion	1 teaspoon garlic granules

Fry the ground sirloin in a large skillet until it's crumbly and no longer pink. Pour off any excess fat. Add the tomatoes and dry ingredients and bring to a boil. Cover and cook over a low flame for 20 minutes or until the rice is tender.

For a salad course in an edible dish, cut two green peppers in half and take out the seeds. Fill the halves with cottage cheese. Tear off chunks of French bread to dip in a communal saucer of virgin olive oil, and pass out zipper-skinned Temple or Honeybell oranges for dessert.

Dishwashing: 1 skillet, 4 plates, 4 forks, 1 saucer.

Trash: 1 can.

Special tips: Buy a dry-style cottage cheese, which will be easier to eat this way. Bag the rice and the other dry ingredients together at home, so they're ready to throw into the recipe without additional measuring. The sirloin can be precooked at home, frozen until you leave, and kept on ice for up to three days.

Walkaway Taco Salads

6 individual bags tortilla chips   1 6-ounce package shredded
1 can your favorite chili   cheese
Shredded lettuce   Yogurt or sour cream

The trick to these "dishless" salads is the way you cut the bag of tortilla chips. Cut each bag across the top and down one side. Now open it, and you'll see that it forms a widemouthed cone. Open the can of chili and set it in a pan of clean water on the stove. Cover it with foil or a lid, then boil the water until the chili is heated through. After you remove it, you still have a pan of clean, hot water for bathing or dishwashing.

To assemble the salads, stand the wrappers in cans or paper cups or have someone hold them. First, ladle some of the hot chili over the chips, then add shredded lettuce, a tuft of cheese, and a dollop of sour cream. Hand each person a salad and a fork, and dinner's on!

Complete the menu with iced gazpacho made at home, carried on ice, and served in bathroom-sized disposable cups. Roast marshmallows over the campfire for dessert.

Dishwashing: 1 serving spoon, 1 fork per person.

Trash: 1 can, assorted burnable wrappers.

Special tip: Wash, dry and cut up the lettuce at home. Seal it in a plastic bag with a clean dish towel to absorb excess moisture and with plenty of air to provide a cushion so the lettuce doesn't get squashed in the ice chest. It will keep for several days in the cooler. Once dried, the towel is clean and usable. The plastic bag can also be reused.

Sausage Squash Boats

2 acorn squash   1 12-ounce package lean
Maple syrup   sausage

Cut the squash in half and discard the seeds. Stuff each half-squash with one-fourth of the sausage. Place sausage-side down on four pieces of foil, bring up the ends, and twist to form a seal. Place flat-side down on a grill over well-started coals and bake 30–45

Use edible dishes such as green pepper halves, pita bread, or ice cream cones.
Jarlsberg Cheese

minutes or until the squash is tender and the sausage well done. Open the foil, drizzle with maple syrup, and serve.

To go with the meal, pass out bread-and-butter sandwiches and big spears of seeded, fresh cucumber to dip into a yogurt-dill sauce. For dessert, pass around long licorice whips and use them for a knot-tying lesson before you eat them.

Dishwashing: 4 forks.

Trash: Plastic sausage wrapper, 4 wads foil.

Special tip: Make plenty of bread-and-butter sandwiches in advance and package them individually so you'll always have bread and butter on hand without having to root out the bread, the butter, and a knife.

Apple Chicken on a Raft

2 tablespoons flour	2 tablespoons butter
1 teaspoon dried parsley flakes	1 tablespoon olive oil
½ teaspoon garlic salt	2 eggs
½ teaspoon paprika	1 cup flour
4 skinless, boned chicken breast halved and slightly flattened	Pinch salt, dash pepper
	4 small Granny Smith apples, cored and halved
1 cup milk	

Before you leave home, measure the two tablespoons of flour and the spices into a gallon-sized plastic bag and seal it well. To assemble the dish, shake the chicken in the bag with the flour mixture until it's well coated. Melt the butter with the olive oil in a roomy skillet (preferably nonstick), and brown the chicken well on all sides. Place two apple halves on each piece of chicken. Cover and let it steam over low flame for 10 minutes.

Place the milk and eggs in a large shaker (such as a peanut jar you were going to discard) and shake to mix. Then add the cup of flour and the seasonings and shake again to form a smooth, thin batter.

Arrange the chicken-apple mounds evenly in the skillet over a medium flame, and pour the batter all at once around and over them. Cover and bake until the pancake is brown and puffy. Cut the pancake into four even portions, each centered with the chicken-apple mound.

Complete this banquet with a centerpiece of fresh broccoli and cauliflower florets around a carton of green onion–sour cream dip. For dessert, bring on individual cans of tapioca pudding you've studded with snipped, dried apricots.

Dishwashing: 1 skillet, 1 spatula, 1 paring knife, 1 serving spoon, 4 plates, 4 knives, 4 forks, 4 spoons.

Trash: Shaker, unless you want to wash and reuse it, 4 pudding cans and lids.

Special tips: Ready-made dips are great time-savers in boat camping, and they're usually labeled with an expiration date. Keep several on hand in the cooler. Wash and cut up the florets at home, and bag them with a clean dish towel to absorb any excess moisture that could hasten discoloration. They'll keep for several days on ice.

Pork Chop Chop

4 lean, meaty pork chops
1 16-ounce package coarsely
  grated cabbage
Salt, pepper to taste

1 16-ounce can German potato
  salad (2 cans if you're big
  eaters)

Brown the pork chops over a hot flame in a roomy skillet. Drain off any excess fat. Top with the grated cabbage, then the potato salad. Cover and simmer over low flame until the chops are cooked through and the cabbage is tender. Divide among four plates.

Complete the picture with chilled whole cranberry sauce plus bread or rolls if you like. Then surprise the crew with a grab bag of individually wrapped desserts such as Moon Pies, Twinkies, or Devil Dogs.

Dishwashing: 1 skillet, 1 serving spoon, 4 plates, 4 knives, 4 forks.

Trash: 1 or 2 cans, some packagings.

Skillet Spapizza

Approx. 2 cups cooked spaghetti	1 6-ounce package pepperoni
2 tablespoons olive oil	(optional)
1 can or jar pizza sauce	1 8-ounce package shredded
1 8-ounce can mushroom slices	mozzarella cheese

Cook the spaghetti at home any time, and seal it in thin layers in a plastic bag. Keep it cold for up to a week, or freeze it for up to two months. To prepare the skillet pizza, press the spaghetti in an even layer in the cold, well-oiled skillet, cutting and chopping if necessary to make an even thickness. Spread with the pizza sauce, sprinkle with the pepperoni and mushrooms (plus any other toppings you like), and top with the cheese. Cover and cook over a medium flame until everything is well heated and the cheese is melted. Cut into four wedges and serve.

Complete the menu with garlic breadsticks and toothpick-a-bob "salads" made by stringing cherry tomatoes and chunks of green pepper on toothpicks. For dessert, give each person a package of Necco wafers and make them last until bedtime while you tell ghost stories around the campfire.

Dishwashing: 1 skillet, 1 spatula, 4 plates, 4 forks.

Trash: 2 cans, some packaging.

Special tips: Make up several cooked spaghetti "forms" at home by freezing batches of leftover spaghetti in pans that are the same diameter as your camp skillet. Then use them as pizza bases.

Crouton Balls

2 cups toasted croutons	1 6-ounce package grated
(homemade or from a package)	cheese
Ketchup or salsa	

Buy your favorite flavor of croutons, or make and season your own. You can also use one of the flavored cheeses, such as pizza or Mexican. Combine the croutons and the cheese in a clean paper bag and toss to mix. Grab handfuls of the mixture and squeeze it into eight balls the size of small eggs. Place a small bowl of ketchup or salsa in the center of the table, and use it as a dip for the crouton balls.

Serve the balls for lunch, with mugs of instant soup and a juicy dessert, such as canned pineapple chunks drained and piled into ice-cream cones.

Dishwashing: 1 bowl, 1 mixing spoon, 4 soup mugs.

Trash: burnable bag, packaging.

Special tip: This works best with a natural cheese rather than aged cheddar or imitation cheeses, which are drier.

Sweet and Sour Onepot

1 16-ounce can sauerkraut
1 16-ounce canned ham
Approx. ⅔ cup water or milk

1 16-ounce can apple-pie
   filling
1½ cups biscuit mix

Empty the sauerkraut into a large skillet. Open the ham and drain the juice into the sauerkraut can. Then add water until the sauerkraut can is half full, and add it to the skillet. Slice the ham without removing it from the can. Arrange the ham slices evenly on top of the sauerkraut. Dapple the pie filling over it all. Add another half-can of water. Put the biscuit mix in the empty ham can and carefully add enough milk to form a thick dough. Mix only until everything is well moistened.

Bring the ham mixture to a low boil, then add the dough by spoonfuls. Keep it boiling slowly for 10 minutes, then add more water if it's too dry and cover tightly. Simmer over a low flame another 10 minutes, and serve at once with a slice of cranberry jelly, rye rolls and butter, and big deli dills.

This is a sweet meal that doesn't really call for dessert, so make popcorn over the campfire later and boil up a kettle of water to make apple-cinnamon tea.

Dishwashing: 1 skillet and lid, 1 mixing spoon, 4 plates, 4 knives, 4 forks, 4 mugs.

Trash: 3 cans.

Special tip: Apple-pie filling contains sugar and spices. If you prefer a more tart result, use pie-sliced apples, which are unsweetened apples with no spices added.

Skillet Frittata

¼ cup virgin olive oil
3 or 4 potatoes
2 or 3 carrots
1 medium onion
1 8-ounce can cut green beans,
   drained

6 eggs
Salt, pepper
6–8 ounces smoked Gouda
   cheese

Thinly slice the potatoes, carrots, and onion. Warm the olive oil in a large nonstick skillet, and sauté the vegetables until lightly browned. Cover and steam over low flame until they're just tender. Add green beans. Shake the eggs with the salt and pepper (or use a seasoned-salt mixture) in a jar until they're airy, then pour over the vegetable mixture and dot with chunks of the smoked cheese (to give the dish a meaty, bacon-like flavor). Cover and bake over a low flame until the eggs are set. Cut into wedges.

Complete this meal with buttered crispbread and kosher dill pickles. For dessert, bring out apple wedges and a carton of caramel dipping sauce.

Dishwashing: 1 skillet (should wipe clean with a paper towel), 1 paring knife, 1 server or 1 spatula, 1 shaker jar (unless it's one you have saved to be disposable), 4 plates, 4 forks.

Trash: Small can, cheese wrapper, egg shells.

Special tips: Scrub the potatoes and carrots at home, dry them well, and wrap them in clean paper towels. In camp simply slice them, unpeeled, into the skillet. Save the paper towels for another use.

15
The Path to the Bath

Showers and Baths

In a boat-camping situation where you're swimming every day or camping each night in parks with hot showers, bathing is less of a problem than it is when you're boat camping along icy streams or in salt water. Here are some wrinkles and dodges that may work for you.

• An innovative showerless shower product is N–O–Dor, made by Sno Seal and sold in sporting-goods shops. Add a small packet of the liquid to a pint of water, using the pump spray bottle that comes with the kit. When you can't shower, spray N–O–Dor on sweaty areas as a refresher. The company suggests that you sleep with the bottle in your sleeping bag so it will be warm when you want to use it in the morning. It's especially refreshing if you feel sticky after bathing in seawater.

• Gravity-fed solar showers, such as Sun Shower, are available from camping- and boating-supply houses. Fill the bag from any available water source and hang it in the rigging or in a tree to warm in the sun. When you're ready, stand under the bag and open the sprayer. We've also used these bags, with their convenient off–on valves, to rinse dishes.

• A clean, new garden sprayer can deliver a pressure shower. (Don't use an old one that has been used for garden pesticides.) Heat water on the stove, fill the reservoir, pump up the pressure, and press the trigger.

Sun Shower holds six gallons of water, enough for one long shower or two or more Navy-style showers. Heat the bag in the sun, then open the sprayer to shower in the warm water. *Basic Designs, Inc.*

Heat water on the stove or in the sun, then put it in a clean garden sprayer. You'll have a pressure shower. *Gordon Groene*

• Create a one-time solar shower by putting a gallon or two of water into a sturdy, dark garbage bag. Hang it in the sun. When it's warm enough, position yourself underneath and stab it in three or four spots with an ice pick. Instant shower! To make sure you won't run out of water before rinsing off all the soap, make the first stabs a few inches up from the bottom of the bag. When the flow stops, a reserve is still in the bag. To drain it, make the last punctures at the lowest point. The bag can then be used for dry trash.

• If freshwater is in short supply and you must bathe in seawater, rub down afterwards with a washcloth rinsed out in freshwater with a little rubbing alcohol. Talcum powder will also help to take away the stickiness.

• If you're boat camping with small children, take along an inflatable wading pool to provide a bathtub and a play pool. It also makes a spacious laundry tub. Ours is only 36 inches in diameter and is easily inflated by mouth.

A small, inflatable swimming pool makes a good bathtub for baby.
Gordon Groene

You won't have to juggle soap and washcloths to bathe children if you "war paint" dirty faces, hands, and knees with shaving cream. *Gordon Groene*

• Small children can't always manage soap and washcloths. Instead, "war paint" them with shaving foam before sending them into the shower for a rinse.

• Older children and adults can manage soap and washcloths. That is, they manage to leave them behind! To avoid losing these costly items, you can provide shower-bound family members with plastic sandwich bags into which generous dabs of a bath gel have been squeezed. Once they have wet themselves down, they can turn their bag soap-side out, use it as a shower mitt, and then discard it in the rest-room rubbish. This method not only prevents loss but also eliminates the smelly problem of washcloths that never quite dry out.

• If you'll be using public showers, wear rubber sandals to keep from picking up athlete's foot. Take along small, sample-sized spray cans of antibacterial, antifungal sanitizers.

• Each person should have his or her own big bath bag, with room to carry a shaving kit or cosmetic bag, a towel, and a change of clothes. A canvas ice carrier is good, or sew shopping-bag-sized carriers of duck or denim. Many public showers provide no clean, dry place to arrange one's gear. If you have your own roomy bag with handles you can hang it on any handy hook, nail, or branch and keep everything clean and dry.

• Keep beach towels separate from bath towels. After a shower, you don't want to put salt and sand back on your body.

• If your boat has a pressurized water system, hook up a water line to a telephone shower head or a sink sprayer in the cockpit or near the boarding platform on the transom. Use it for after-swim rinses.

• Moist towelettes are convenient, but to carry enough for a long cruise would be expensive and would create a great deal of trash. Start out each day with a clean, wet washcloth sealed in a plastic sandwich bag. Use it for wiping hands and faces. Hang it up each night to dry, and wash it out each morning to start fresh again.

• Color code towels and washcloths, buying a different color for each person, so each family member knows his or her own.

• It takes little time or sewing skill to stitch small strips of Velcro onto a bath towel or a beach towel in spots that will allow you to wear it as a sarong or wraparound skirt. Self-stick Velcro patches can be put on any available bulkhead or tent wall to serve as a rack for the towel. The Velcro closure can also be used to wrap the towel around a clothesline without clothespins.

• In cold-weather camping, consider carrying medium-weight terry robes for everyone aboard. In many marinas and campgrounds hot water is in short supply, and shower rooms may not be heated at all. Hop out of the shower and into the robe instead of shivering through a towel rubdown. The robes are no more bulky to carry than an equal amount of terry towels, and they double as both towel and garment. Heavy-weight terry would be more absorbent and warmer, but it takes so long to dry that it's not always practical in boat camping. Ours are simple, homemade caftans made out of towels from a discount store.

Toilets

All of us want to be environmentally responsible, but there are times in the outback when we simply must leave more than footprints. Some boat-camping adventures are too long to get by on one small holding tank and too remote to provide pump-outs or other "civilized" alternatives.

In some areas where population pressures have become overwhelming, such as the Grand Canyon, every bit of human waste must be packed out. In others, where there are no official guidelines or mandates, let your conscience be your guide.

Elimination is the most necessary part of boat camping but the most unlovely to discuss. If your boat is large enough to have a head aboard, you have one set of problems. If you must go ashore, you have another set. Some boat campers still swear by the old oaken bucket; others, the pit toilet. Still others prefer the fancy new compact, portable flush toilets that must be emptied ashore once a day or so.

We've tried them all, from homemade buckets to high-tech marine toilets. One of the best was homemade and cost nothing. We took a large metal bucket and cut out a sturdy wooden seat that fit securely over it. The bucket, which never got dirty because it was always completely lined with plastic bags, could also be used as a catchall or as a scrub bucket. The seat stored flat and could be stashed elsewhere.

We would put a plastic bag into the bucket, drape it over the top, and clamp it in place by adding the seat. After each bag was used it was sealed with a rubber band and removed to a large garbage bag. Because everything was well sealed, there was never any odor. When we went ashore, the waste could be buried or dropped down a pit toilet. We also found that a bag thrown onto a roaring bonfire simply vanished—no steam, no odor, no residue.

To horrified environmentalists, we point out that we were miles from any other camps or campers. The only other choice would have been to do as we knew some others were doing: empty the mess overboard on the sneak.

In undeveloped areas you can just take off for the woods when nature calls, dig a hole, and use it. Or you can choose a secluded spot to be the communal bathroom and make a trench toilet. With a camp shovel, dig a narrow trench a foot or two deep and several feet long. Remove the sod layer in undisturbed chunks, if possible, so you can replace it when you fill in the trench. Start using the trench at one end, shoveling dirt over each used portion. As you work from one end of the trench to the other, it is gradually filled in and returned to its natural state.

If you have a recirculating toilet that uses chemicals, buy only the most environmentally safe, biodegradable products so you won't be burying poisons or adding them to campground septic systems. Some can actually kill the bacteria that keep the septic tank "alive," and soon an entire campground is without a sewage system.

One formaldehyde-free toilet treatment we like is Instant Fresh, made by Starbrite. It damps odors, helps to break down waste, and has special lubricants that help keep the plumbing healthy. It comes in several scents and can be used in holding tanks, recirculating toilets, or portable toilets. Read the manufacturer's directions.

Where shoreside facilities have been provided, of course, one uses them. It's much easier to walk down the dock to use the bathroom in the marina or campground than to have to empty, clean, and refill a recirculating toilet or to empty and flush out a holding tank. Don't forget to have a supply of toilet paper with you. In public toilets it's usually all gone, festooned all over the cubicle, or as harsh as sandpaper.

For day use on board, portable urinals are available in several forms. For emergency (one-time) use, one of the best is called a Convenience Bag. The bags are sold in marinas and at general-aviation airports for about a dollar each. If you can't find them, call GKR Industries, Inc. at 708–389–2003 and ask where they're sold in your city. Filled, the disposable bag is leakproof.

For regular use buy a reusable plastic portable urinal with a leakproof top (a female adapter is available). One source is Gander Mountain (800–558–9410), a camping-catalog house; another is the J. L. Pachner catalog, obtainable by writing to the company at 13 Via Di Nola, Laguna Niguel, California 92677.

16
Coming Clean

There's no escape from the chores that go with living day-to-day. Sand grinds into tent floors and cabin soles. Crumbs fall. The waterline develops a mustache. In dusty areas, screens clog. In salt spume, windscreens turn filmy. Grime builds up in seats. Bedding becomes dank. Laundry gets mildewed and smells worse every day.

Half the battle is to start out with clean gear, preferably gear that has been chosen for its ease of cleanup, such as the best-quality nonstick cookware and washable sleeping bags with removable liners. The other half of the battle is to keep one step ahead of the dirt, allotting some time each day to unwelcome—but necessary—cleaning.

Keeping It Clean

Any dirt you can keep out of the boat or tent is dirt you don't have to shovel out later. Where possible, develop the habit of slipping out of your shoes before you enter your boat cabin or tent. This works well for us in some boats but not so well in others. It's more important when we're in muddy or sandy areas than when we're stepping onto the boat from a clean dock or entering the tent from a cement pad.

Grid soles on deck shoes and athletic shoes can hold bushels of dirt. No matter how thoroughly you wipe and scrape your feet before you board the boat, these soles drop tons of dirt each time they're flexed. Wear deck shoes for safe footing under way, but you'll save a lot of sweeping if you wear smooth soles ashore.

Make use of whatever doormat(s) you can manage at as many places as possible: before boarding the boat, between the cockpit and the cabin, in front of the tent, and so on. If all you can manage is an old chenille rug, or even a thick towel, it will scrape sand and grit off your feet and will shake clean in seconds. Yet it will take up very little space when it's folded and stowed.

Wooden grating also makes a good doormat, both ashore and afloat. If your cockpit sole is teak grating, you can simply take it ashore to use as a "welcome mat" at the tent door and as a grating to stand on when you take a solar shower under a tree. As a doormat it allows sand to fall through; as a grating it can be used to keep things high and dry with good air circulation. Folding, portable teak gratings for shower and doormat use are sold through camping and marine catalogs.

Rubbery, fatigue-mat-type decking squares are a boon to any boat and are a double boon to boat camping because the interlocking squares can be reconfigured day after day to suit your needs on deck, on the bottom of a canoe, in the boat's cabin, or in the campsite. The decking is about the best antiskid surface you can find, and, because it is full of holes, it allows dirt and liquids to fall through. Things can be extremely messy, yet you're still walking on a fairly clean, dry mat. Pull it up for cleaning when you have a spare moment.

Crumbs create a cleaning problem but, even worse, they attract bugs and rodents. It's a good idea to designate certain areas for eating; others for sleeping.

Keep salt water away from bunks, bedding, and bath towels. It leaves a residue that may dry during the heat of the day but attracts moisture back out of the air at night. As a result fabrics feel damp and skin feels slimy.

Use nonstick cookware, which wipes clean with paper toweling or rags. Add stainproofers/waterproofers to fabrics. Silicone Water-Guard, which is 10 percent silicone compared to the 2–5 percent found in most supermarket spray-on protectants, can be used on leathers and suedes as well as on cottons and canvas. For information call 800–845–2728.

In most instances keeping things clean also involves keeping them dry and well aired so they don't develop mildew, which eats fibers and ruins fabrics. Says Ken Kearns of Eureka! Tents, "Hang it from the clothesline. Hang it from the garage rafters. Hang it from a tree. Hang your tent anywhere you can...but *store it dry.*"

During the trip, do everything you can to avoid stowing a wet tent.

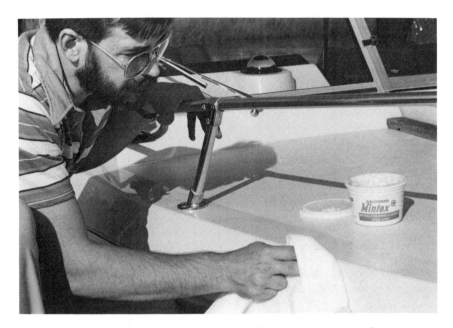

Waterless hand cleaner does many jobs around the boat and camp, from cleaning a greasy waterline "mustache" to washing dirty hands and knees. The cleaner works at body temperature, so rub it in with your hands until cleaning is complete. Then wipe (or rinse) clean. *Savogran*

When possible, start out later in the day, after the morning sun has dried the dew. Open all the vents so the tent can air out and dry while you eat breakfast. If the top is thoroughly dry, throw it over a clothesline so the bottom can dry too. Each evening pitch the tent as soon as possible after you find a campsite, and allow breezes to flow through and freshen it.

Getting It Clean

Nothing beats a real vacuum cleaner, but most of us don't have the space or the electricity to justify carrying even the smallest electric vacuum cleaner when we go boat camping. Rechargeables aren't much help either, unless you can plug the charger in at least every other day. As for 12-volt vacuum cleaners, most of them are useless.

The trusty old favorites are a whisk broom and a dust pan. If you

Cleaning Shortcuts

- *Use a nonstick pan spray on sticky, stubborn glue that continues to cling after you've removed a price tag or a label. Let the oil soak in, then clean it with detergent and water.*

- *If you have carpeting anywhere in the boat and spill something on it, scoop up as much as possible, then blot the stain repeatedly with clean paper toweling or white rags. If you add water or cleaning fluid, you'll spread the stain; dabbing will drive it into the fibers. The exception is battery acid, which should immediately be sprinkled with baking soda or some other neutralizer.*

- *To clean plastic portlights, windscreens, and hatches, use marine cleaners made specifically for such plastics. If your marina doesn't carry one, try the general-aviation hangar at an airport. Household cleansers can etch or streak these plastics.*

- *Remove last year's decals by swabbing them with white vinegar. Soak them well to soften them, then scrape them very gently. Don't put decals on acrylics.*

- *Coat ballpoint-pen stains on white vinyl upholstery with hair spray, then clean the vinyl by whatever method is recommended for it.*

- *To loosen the oily filth that builds up on stove grates, grills, and other cooking surfaces, seal them in a plastic trash bag with a cup of ammonia. Avoid getting ammonia on your skin or breathing its fumes. Gently slosh the bag around from time to time, and let everything soak several hours or overnight. Rinse the item well, first with a vinegar-and-water solution and then with plain water.*

cut the bottom off a flat-sided, two-quart plastic bottle, it serves as both a dustpan and a bailer. Save an old detergent bottle with a handle; plastic milk jugs aren't strong enough.

Keep cleaning products simple and natural. Most marine stores

More Cleaning Shortcuts

- *Small scorch marks on suede upholstery can usually be removed with a pencil eraser.*

- *If possible, take plastic galleyware home for a scrub in the dishwasher at the end of each boat-camping trip. The high heat and caustic detergent will take out stains and odors that hand dishwashing doesn't dislodge.*

- *Lemon-oil furniture treatment (not furniture polish) is very effective for cleaning wood finishes inside the cabin of your boat, and it also helps to prevent future mildew buildup.*

- *A vegetable brush is the right size and shape for cleaning any small head, and it takes less room than a toilet brush. We made a toilet-brush holder by cutting down a plastic two-liter pop bottle.*

- *Vinyl seat-cushion covers can be washed in an automatic washer. Use warm water, a mild detergent, and add two bath towels to do the scrubbing. Don't overfill the machine. If the covers are bleach safe, add the bleach during the wash cycle. Let the wash water drain, then bypass the spin cycle. Rinse, drain the rinse water, and stop the machine before it spins. Hang the covers inside out until they're almost dry, then replace the fillers and let the cushions stand in a warm, dry place until they're thoroughly dry.*

- *Disinfect cutting boards with a solution of bleach and water. They can be a source of food poisoning when bits of food lodge in the crevices.*

- *Baking soda is not only an effective deodorizer for the icebox, it also is a food-quality abrasive that can be used safely in the galley-on-the-go. Don't use cleansers or steel-mesh pads unless you can rinse them thoroughly with hot water to remove all traces of gritty residue.*

sell all-purpose cleaners that can be used for everything from decks to dishes. Try different brands until you find one that is an effective cleaner but doesn't create oceans of suds. When water is in short supply, it's almost impossible to rinse them away.

Carry plenty of strong nylon line for repairs, lashing, clotheslines, and many other uses. A good clothesline is essential for keeping gear dry and well aired. *Coleman*

Baking soda is one of the best all-purpose cleaning products in boat camping. Add it to wash water to soften it. Use it to deodorize the ice chest, potty, plastic containers. Use it as an abrasive on pots and pans. If food is burned black in a pan, bring some water and baking soda to a boil and the carbon will probably boil loose. One of its best features is that it's a food product. If you must be skimpy with rinse water, you don't have to worry about harmful particles being left behind, as you do with steel wool and gritty cleansers.

Another of our favorite get-tough cleaners is a waterless hand cleaner. Used around the house and shop, it removes paint and grease from your hands yet doesn't harm your skin. It's especially good for cleaning greasy buildup off pans and the stove. It depends on body heat to make it work, so keep rubbing it in until the grease softens. Then flush it away with water.

Laundry

On short trips you can simply let laundry accumulate until you get home. However, on longer trips and in flyweight boat camping where you have only one or two changes of clothes and must wash out a few things each day, laundry is a fact of life.

We've washed clothes in tubs as small as a collapsible bucket and as large as our entire eight-foot inflatable boat. After an all-night rain filled it with sweet, soft water, we jumped in for our first freshwater baths in weeks, then did the laundry in it. Moral: the cleaner you keep the inside of a boat, the cleaner the catch you'll have if some act of Providence fills it with rainwater.

A 36-inch inflatable wading pool from the discount store makes a great basin for large laundry items, such as bath towels or sleeping-bag liners. A bucket just isn't roomy enough. Carry a washboard or a small toilet plunger to agitate the laundry.

You can also "vibrate" the clothes clean if you have enough room on board to carry a small plastic trash can with a lid that locks on. Use it as your clothes hamper. When it's about half filled with dirty clothes, add water and detergent, clamp the lid on, secure the can with shock-cord or wedge it in securely, and let it jounce away as you cruise to tonight's campsite.

When you arrive, wring and rinse a few times, and things are ready to hang out to dry. Don't overdo the wringing, by the way—it's highly destructive to fabrics. It's better to allow more drip-drying time.

Bring a concentrated liquid detergent and be sure to dilute it according to directions on the bottle before you add clothes. Powdered concentrates don't dissolve as easily, especially in cold or hard water. If you can manage a small bottle of rinse concentrate to use as a last step in hand washing, you can freshen and soften fabrics that otherwise might not be as soft and sweet as machine washing could make them.

We also carry a small "stain stick," to treat stains before items are put into laundry bags. The stained items can then be dumped into the first available bucket or coin laundry without further treatment.

In a pinch we have often laundered clothes and linens in salt or brackish water, but they always feel damp afterward unless we can give them a thorough final rinse in freshwater. Avoid saltwater laundering if possible.

The best clothesline in the flyweight class is a braid made from three strands of rubber tubing. It's available from Magellan's or from Flexo-Line, Box 162, Dunbridge, Ohio 43414. It has loops on each end and can be stretched up to seven feet between two trees or between two hooks in a boat. No clothespins are needed because corners of fabric are tucked into the braid, which grips them firmly. The line can hold up to 12 pounds of wet garments or towels.

We've also dried clothes on lifelines and by running them up the halyard. For this, use plenty of good wooden clothespins. Cheaper plastic pins snap in high winds. Even the wooden ones should be watched closely when conditions are windy; items pull loose and are lost overboard.

No matter what else we carry as a clothesline, we have on hand at least 75–100 feet of strong, compact ¼-inch nylon line. In addition to being great for hanging clothes and gear, the line can be used for lashing down supplies, bundling up gear, rigging sun flies, and much more.

With luck, you'll sometimes put into marinas that have coin-operated laundry machines. Keep a good supply of coins on hand. You need a dryer most when you come into port soaking wet in the middle of the night. And that's the time when nobody is around to make change.

Don't trust your sleeping bag or any other expensive item to a washer and dryer you haven't tried before. Our list of horror stories about commercial washers is a long one. In one instance, we set a machine for a cold-water wash and soon noticed steam coming out of it—the hoses had been reversed! And that water wasn't just hot, it was scalding.

We can suggest a screwball way to minimize laundry: throw things away after they're soiled! For weeks before a trip we save items that are good for one more wearing or use: frayed underwear, bedding, and towels; socks that are going thin at the heels and toes; last year's jeans. You may also have things that the children are right on the edge of outgrowing.

As you pack, incorporate these disposables into your planning. This isn't to say that you all have to look like ragamuffins, but there is a last time for everything and this may as well be it. The more rugged your boat-camping life, the more chance of losing garments overboard, of holing or staining a good outfit, or of leaving a good jacket behind in a remote campsite. Why risk an entirely new wardrobe on a wilderness trip where you won't see anybody but each other?

An Ode to Trash Bags

It's almost impossible to carry too many trash bags—the larger and sturdier, the better. Use them to corral trash and seal away its bad smells. Use clean, flat trash bags as ground covers and "table" cloths. Use plastic bags to keep things separate and dry. It's almost impossible to have too many.

We haven't found twist-tie closures to be dependable enough for the rough handling these bags get in boat camping, so we buy drawstring bags and also carry lots of rubber bands. When smelly loads have to be stored, don't wait for the entire bag to be full. Seal each level with a new rubber band, and scatter a little baking soda in the clean, dry, remaining part of the bag. The result will be a huge sausage, tied at intervals—funny looking but much sweeter smelling.

If you have enough space to carry a separate trash can with a tight-fitting lid, so much the better. If you'll be taking the can ashore, make that a locking lid. A press-fit, no matter how tight, is a pushover for bears and raccoons.

A thin layer of newspaper in the bottom of the can helps to absorb odors and leaks. Scatter baking soda in the can too. On some pack-it-out trips, we've had to carry refuse for as long as two weeks before we could find a place to dispose of it properly.

17
Blue Water, Green Planet

We boat campers can make ourselves at home anywhere in the outdoors, ashore or asea. So, because the outdoors is our home, we can't draw the curtain against debris. We have a big stake in keeping the earth green and the water blue. Here are some ways to make your boating, camping, and boat camping cleaner and kinder to the environment:

Boating Etiquette

- Don't make wakes. They endanger other boaters and damage fragile shorelines.

- Secure trash on board where it can't be blown or thrown overboard. Only boats 26 feet and longer are required by the U.S. Coast Guard to display a garbage-disposal placard, but boats of all sizes should observe the same precautions about trash. It is illegal to dump trash or garbage in U.S. waters.

- Observe fishing laws and limits even in the most remote areas where enforcement is unlikely.

- If you're leaving oil sheen on the water, you're in violation of federal law. Fix leaks. Keep an absorbent oil "pillow" handy in case oil spills into the bilge. If you have a bilge pump, fit it with an oil-filtration attachment.

- If you have a potty on board, dispose of its contents in pump-out stations or campground rest rooms. Use only earth-safe chemicals or deodorants in it, or none at all.

- If you wash the boat on or near the water, use biodegradable soaps. If you scrape the bottom, get well away from the water and spread newspapers or tarps under the boat to catch the fallout. Scrapings from bottom paints can be toxic; scrapings of marine growths from one waterway can introduce them into another waterway.

- Winterize with earth-friendly antifreezes rather than with ethylene glycol products.

- Dispose of all chemicals, batteries, and hazardous materials in containers provided by marinas for that purpose. Some are saved for recycling; others must be disposed of in specified ways.

Camping Etiquette

- Shop for items that will reduce trash. They include reusable tableware instead of disposables, powdered drink mixes instead of canned or bottled drinks, and dried foods, such as rice, instead of bulky convenience items.

- Minimize the use of paper towels and wiping cloths by bringing along a stuff bag filled with clean cotton or linen rags. When they're clean, use them to wipe up food-preparation areas, then demote them to engine or deck rags before you discard them.

- Don't "donate" cooking or washup water to wild plants. It could do more harm than good if it is hot or if it contains salt or chemicals.

- Use biodegradable soaps for cleaning the boat, the camp, the dishes, and yourself. Sport-Wash for outdoor specialty fabrics, including wool and down, and Sport-Wash Hair and Body Soap come in tubes and contain no scents or other noncleaning additives, so they rinse with minimal water. For ordering information, call 800–845–2728 or 803–531–1820.

- Observe fire-building codes, which may change from day to day according to forest conditions.

- Use only dead wood for fires. Don't damage trees by girdling them with ropes, hacking off branches or pieces of bark for kindling, or blazing them to mark a trail. That's Hollywood stuff, not twentieth-century good-citizenship.

- If the campground provides recycling bins, sort your discards carefully. Sorting requirements may be different from the categories you use at home.

- Leave campground toilets, sinks, and showers as clean as or cleaner than you found them.

- Don't put noncombustibles in the campfire. Rake the fire pit completely clean of any residual foil, metal, or glass and pack it out.

- Don't harvest more than your share, afloat or ashore.

- Challenge your family to leave a campsite looking as good as or better than it did when you arrived. It becomes a game after a while, one that gives more and more pleasure as your skills improve. You might, for example, send the children on a "trashure" hunt while you weave a small garland of dead pine needles to leave in the fire ring as a gift of tinder to the next camper.

Sources and Resources

America Outdoors, P. O. Box 1348, Knoxville, Tennessee 37902 (615–524–4814) publishes a directory of outfitters that rent canoes, rafts, jet boats, and kayaks on some of America's most exciting waterways. Also listed are instructors and guided, completely outfitted boat-camping packages.

Members of **Boat/U.S.,** 880 Pickett Street, Alexandria, Virginia 22304 receive discounts on products, insurance, and services. The catalog is one of the best sources of marine and camping equipment. The most effective boating organization in the nation, it is a powerful lobbyist on behalf of boating rights.

Camping World stores are located throughout the United States. If you can't find one near you, call 800–626–5944 to request a catalog. The company has one of the most comprehensive stocks of camping and RV gear in the nation.

Courseline provides information on finding a course on operating a boat (call 800–336–BOAT; in Virginia, 800–245–BOAT) or on learning to sail (800–447–4700). Courses in boating skills are also offered by some chapters of the American Red Cross.

Disabled Outdoors magazine, 2052 West 23rd Street, Chicago, Illinois 60608 covers recreation, including boating, camping, and fishing, for the disabled.

The **Gander Mountain** catalog house specializes in boating and camping supplies. Call 800–558–9410 or write to the company at Box 248, Highway W, Wilmot, Wisconsin 53192.

Request a free catalog from **Magellan's,** Box 5485, Santa Barbara, California 93150, or call 800–962–4943. The company carries unusual travel aids, many of them essential for the boat camper.

Oars, Box 67, Angels Camp, California 95222 (209–736–4677) outfits boat-camping trips aboard rafts and kayaks on white-water rivers in the West, in Alaska, and abroad.

J. L. Pachner Ltd., 13 Via Di Nola, Laguna Niguel, California 92677 will send you a free catalog of adaptive equipment that makes boating and camping easier for the disabled.

Patagonia Mail Order, Box 8900, Bozeman, Montana 59715 is a source of specialized sportswear.

The **Real Goods,** 966 Mazzoni Street, Ukiah, California 95482–3479 (800–762–7325) catalog house offers hard-to-find solar, propane, and 12-volt supplies for boat camping "off the grid"—that is, with no shore power.

Skipper's Course, a home-study course in boat operation, is available from the U.S. Government Bookstore, World Savings Building, 720 North Main Street, Pueblo, Colorado 81003 (719–544–3142). Ask for stock item #050012002258.

Travel Medicine, Inc. sells hard-to-find products having to do with travel health, including insect repellents, several styles of mosquito netting, water filters, and sunscreens. Call 800–872–8633 for a free catalog.

Uncommon Adventures, Box 6066, East Lansing, Michigan 48826 offers wilderness workshops and services, including outfitting, expeditions, and planning for canoe and sea-kayak tours.

The **U.S. Coast Guard Boating Safety Hotline** is 800–368–5647.

Index

several Flashlights Big One
Sports Auth
cell phone   Garb Bags
Lantern, fuel
Tools   coleman stove
Knife
Gear Bags   Stove
gore tex pants   Matches   camp sta
w -proof spray   Radio
    xtra line